Delicious Brazilian Recipes for Authentic Cuisine

Alex H. Duke

Delicious Brazilian Recipes for Authentic Cuisine : Savor the Flavors of Brazil with These Mouthwatering Authentic Recipes

Funny helpful tips:

Invest in long-term strategies; they provide direction and stability.

Embrace change; it's the only constant, and adaptability is a strength.

Introduction

This is a culinary journey into the vibrant and diverse flavors of Brazil, offering a delightful array of dishes to tantalize your taste buds. Here's what you can expect to find within its pages:

Discover the richness of Brazilian cuisine and the cultural influences that shape its unique flavors. From indigenous traditions to Portuguese, African, and immigrant influences, Brazilian food reflects the country's rich heritage and diversity.

Explore the diverse regions of Brazil and their culinary specialties, from the Amazon Rainforest to the beaches of Rio de Janeiro, the pampas of the South, and the bustling streets of São Paulo.

Start your day with a taste of Brazil's breakfast delights, from hearty tapioca pancakes and savory cheese bread to tropical fruit bowls and rich Brazilian coffee.

Whet your appetite with an enticing selection of Brazilian appetizers, featuring classics like Coxinha (chicken croquettes), Pão de Queijo (cheese bread), and Pastéis (fried turnovers) filled with various savory fillings.

Freshen up your meal with vibrant Brazilian salads, showcasing colorful vegetables, fruits, and traditional ingredients like hearts of palm and black beans.

Warm up with comforting Brazilian soups, including the famous Feijoada (black bean stew), Caldo Verde (kale soup), and Canja de Galinha (chicken and rice soup).

Indulge in the bold flavors of Brazilian main dishes, such as Moqueca (fish stew), Feijão Tropeiro (bean and sausage dish), Picanha (grilled beef), and Acarajé (black-eyed pea fritters).

Save room for dessert and explore the sweet side of Brazilian cuisine with treats like Brigadeiro (chocolate truffles), Quindim (coconut flan), and Pudim de Leite (caramel custard).

Quench your thirst with refreshing Brazilian drinks, including Caipirinha (a cocktail made with cachaça, lime, and sugar), Guarana (a popular soda), and fresh fruit juices.

Whether you're a seasoned chef or a curious home cook, this book invites you to experience the vibrant flavors and rich culinary traditions of Brazil right in your own kitchen.

Contents

Why Brazilian Cuisine? 1

Tapioca Crepes With Cheese 6

Brazilian French Toast (Rabanada)..7

Egg Custard (Bom-Boca do) 9

Brazilian Hash Scramble 11

Brazilian Garlic Cheese Bread (PaoDe Queijo) 12

Morning Rice Pudding..14

Brazilian Bread 15

Brazilian Passion Fruit Smoothie 16

Brazilian Avocado Smoothie..18

Brazilian Sandwich 19

Baked Eggs..21

Toasted Manioc Flour Meal (Farofa DeOvo E Cebolinha) 23

Brazilian Dough Balls 24

Brunch Omelet 25

Beans With Fried Bacon AndScrambled Eggs 26

Brazilian Cheese Eggs Benedict..27

Brazilian Savory Pancakes 28

Brazilian Muffins...29

Brazilian Acai Bowl..30

Acarajé 31

Shrimp Tapioca Crepes (Tapioca ComCamarão No Dendê) 33

Brazilian Chicken Croquettes(Coxinha) 35

Grilled Cheese Sticks 37

Brazilian Pasties With Chicken (PastelFrito De Frango) 38

Brazilian Quindim 40

Brazilian Cream Cheese (Requeijão)...41

Brazilian Beef Pastel 42

Hearts Of Palm Pastel...44

Cheese Pastel...46

Brazilian Chicken Wings..47

Gaucho Potato Salad 48

Brazilian Seafood Salad 49

Colorful Avocado Salad 50

Brazilian Potato Salad 51

Brazilian Kale Salad 52

Brazilian Chicken Salad (Salpicão DeFrango) 53

Brazilian Onion Salad..54

Brazilian Hearts Of Palm Salad 55

Brazilian Tomato Slaw 56

Brazilian Chopped Salad 57

Black-Eyed Peas Tuna Salad 58

Tuna Salad 59

Brazilian Shrimp Soup...60

Brazilian Black Bean Soup 61

Brazilian Chicken And Rice Soup...63

Brazilian Lentil Soup With Kale 65

Brazilian Turkey Soup...66

Feijoada Soup 68

Brazilian Sausage Kale Soup..69

Tomato Soup With Eggs 70

Chicken Noodle Soup 71

Green Cabbage Soup 72

Sausage Kidney Bean Soup 73

Kale And Cabbage Soup..74

Fish Soup 76

Macaroni Bean Soup...78

Chicken Soup (Canja De Galinha) 79

Brazilian Fish Stew (Moqueca) 81

Chicken Fricassee With ShoestringPotatoes 83

Cod In Cheese Sauce (Bacalao QuatroQueijos)..............................84

Picanha Roast 86

Brazilian Corn Chowder (Sopa DeMilho Verde)...............................87

Brazilian Minestrone..88

Macarronada Com Requeijão(Brazilian Mac And Cheese)........................89

Pizza A Portuguesa..91

Brazilian Beans 92

Skirt Steak...93

Cold Chicken Sandwich (SanduícheNatural De Frango) 94

Brazilian Pork Ribs (Costela De PorcoAssada) 95

Pan Fried Collard Greens (Couve AMineira)..97

Ham And Cheese Baked Rice 98

Brazilian Chicken Pot Pie...99

Brazilian Saffron Rice With Chicken(Galinhada) 101

Creamy Corn Gratin (Creme De MilhoGratinado).....................................103

Brazilian Potato Cod Casserole 104

Brazilian Pork Stew 106

Brazilian Clams 108

Shrimp Stew...109

Brazilian Beef Stew 110

Seafood Bread Stew 112

Brazilian Shrimp Fry..113

Chicken Sausage Rice..114

Brazilian Beef Skewers 116

Brazilian Rice And Beans..117

Brazilian Beef Roast..118

Brazilian Beef Steaks 119

Brazilian Glazed Chicken 120

Wine Garlic Pork 122

Braised Chicken...123

Corn Bundt Cake (Bolo De Milho DeLiquidificador) 124

Papaya Cream With Cassis (Creme DePapaya Com Cassis) 125

Tapioca Breadsticks (Biscoito DePolvilho) 126

Apple Crumb Cake 127

Bread Pudding (Pudim De Pão)..129

Brazilian Carrot Cake 130

Brigadeiro Cookies 132

No Bake Tapioca Cake 133

Brazilian Coconut Kisses (BeijinhosDe Coco)........................134

Avocado Mousse 135

Brazilian Cornmeal Cake 136

Moist Coconut Cake...137

Chocolate Covered Cream Pie 139

Brazilian Flan 141

Brazilian Fudge Balls (TraditionalBrigadeiros).......................142

Brazilian Cream Doughnuts 143

Passion Fruit Mousse...145

Caipirinha Cocktail 146

Strawberry Caipirinha...147

Brazilian Lemonade 148

Brazilian Strawberry Drink..149

Brazilian Sunrise Cocktail 150

Why Brazilian Cuisine?

The Brazilian cuisine has a combination of several cooking traditions and practices, which are deeply influenced from European, African, Amerindian, and Asian cuisines. Since Brazil is a geographically diverse piece of land, covering a large area, it has several regional cuisines that are termed collectively as Brazilian cuisine. In other words, there's no single national Brazilian cuisine, rather, a mixture of culinary influences which the country received from its past over the centuries. Among the various regional cuisines include:

Southeast Brazilian cuisine: In this region, falls areas exist like Esparto Santo, Sao Paulo and Rio de Janeiro. Consuming rice and beans are quite popular. Dishes like Feidjoh are very famous in this region. Seafood is another major food enjoyed by the people living in the south eastern part of the country. The use of shrimp in snacks, entrees, and other meals is quite common in Minas Garius. Most of the popular dishes are prepared using traditional cheeses, chicken, beans, pork, and corn.

North Brazil: The northern region of the country has states like Amazonas, Acre, etc. And the use of cassava and cassava flour is highly common in this region. Similarly, raw ground maniac root is heavily used in the north Brazilian cuisine.

Then features the central Brazilian cuisine, the Northeast, Eastern, and Southern cuisines, in which you'll taste recipes with, crabs, shrimp, seafood, rice, beans, and chicken. There are a number of other recipes that can be termed as Brazilian specialties. Some of the popular meals from the country feature:

- Cod in Cheese Sauce (Bacalhau Quatro Queijos)
- Brazilian Corn Chowder (Sopa De Milho Verde)

- Brazilian Minestrone
- Macarronada Com Requeijão (Brazilian Mac And Cheese)
- Pizza A Portuguesa
- Brazilian Beans

In desserts, there are several good options to choose:

- Corn Bundt Cake (Bolo De Milho De Liquidificador)
- Papaya Cream With Cassis (Creme De Papaya Com Cassis)
- Bread Pudding (Pudim De Pão)
- Brazilian Carrot Cake
- Brigadeiro Cookies

Let's see the other interesting Brazilian meals in this cookbook that you can easily cook at home.

Brazil

The Federative Republic of Brazil or Brazil is one of the largest countries of Latin and South America. It has the population of 211 million people, making it the sixth most populous country in the region. Brazil is the most ethnically diverse and multicultural country with people belonging to different origins from around the world. Eastern Brazil has the Atlantic Ocean with a coastline of 4,655 miles (7,491 km). It almost covers half of the landmass of South America. So, its border touches all the countries of South America, except for Chile and Ecuador. The country has the amazing Amazon Basin, which has vast stretches of tropical forest, a very diverse wildlife, and several ecosystems with different habitats and that make it the one of the most mega diverse nations in the world.

Before the 1500s, Brazil was home to several tribal nations. However, in 1500, the Portuguese Empire took over and ruled the region until 1822. Brazil gained its independence in 1822 and became the Empire of Brazil. The word "Brazil" itself comes from the Portuguese word called "Brazil wood," a tree grown on the Brazilian coast. In the Portuguese language, this Brazil wood is also known as *Pau Brasil*.

Brazil covers a huge land along the eastern coast of South America, and it shares its borders with Uruguay in the south, Argentina and Paraguay, in the southwest, Bolivia and Peru in the West, Colombia, in the Northwest, and French Guiana, Suriname in the north. It has number of oceanic archipelagos which have different names, such as Paul rocks, Fernando de Noronha, etc.

Brazil is geographically quite diverse and serves as the 5th largest country in the world. The topography of Brazil includes hills, mountains, scrublands, highlands, and plains. The upland area covers the southern half of the country; in contrast, plateaus are present in the north western side of the country. Its southeastern part consists of rugged mountain ranges. Northern country has highlands; and the Amazon Basin is present in the South. Brazil comprises several weather conditions according to its topography. It has six major climatic subtypes, including subtropical, oceanic, semi-arid, tropical, equatorial, and desert.

Tourism is a booming sector in Brazil and the major contributing industry for the economy. In 2015, around 6.36 million people visited the country. It's truly one of the major tourist attractions in South and Latin America. Due to its natural areas, and spot attracting most of the tourists from around the world. The popular destinations in Brazil include the Amazon, Amazon rainforest, the dunes and beaches of now North East region beaches at Rio de Janeiro. Santa Catarina, in the center West region. The competitive advantages for the Brazilian tourism industry are visible everywhere; and it's one of countries on the planet that's always worth the visit.

Breakfast

Tapioca Crepes With Cheese

Preparation time: 10 minutes
Cook time: 10 minutes
Nutrition facts (per serving): 274 Cal (10g fat, 9g protein, 2.5g fiber)

Without these Tapioca crepes, it seems like the Brazilian breakfast menu is incomplete. Try them with different variations of fillings.

Ingredients (2 servings)
⅓ cup of tapioca flour
1 pinch of salt
3 tablespoons of water
Butter, to spread
½ cup of mozzarella cheese, shredded

Preparation
Blend the tapioca flour with the salt and the water in a bowl until smooth. Set a skillet greased with butter over medium heat. Pour the flour batter in it, spread it around, and cook for 1-2 minutes per side. Transfer the crepe to a suitable plate and top with butter and cheese. Fold this crepe and serve.

Brazilian French Toast (Rabanada)

Preparation time: 10 minutes
Cook time: 10 minutes
Nutrition facts (per serving): 270 Cal (3g fat, 11g protein, 2g fiber)

This Brazilian French toast is an everyday breakfast meal that you should definitely add to your menu. You can try these toasts with eggs and crispy bacon.

Ingredients (4 servings)
¼ cup sugar
1 tablespoon cinnamon
3 cup milk
4 eggs
1 loaf, French bread, sliced
Oil, for frying

Preparation
Mix the cinnamon and the sugar on a plate. Beat the eggs in one bowl and add milk to another. Set a skillet greased with oil. Dip the bread in the milk and then coat with the egg and cook for 2-3 minutes per side. Transfer the French toasted to a plate lined with paper towel. Drizzle cinnamon sugar on top. Serve.

Egg Custard (Bom-Boca do)

Preparation time: 10 minutes
Cook time: 10 minutes
Nutrition facts (per serving): 202 Cal (7g fat, 6g protein, 1.3g fiber)

If you love to have a different variety of morning custard in your breakfast menu, then this egg custard is a must!

Ingredients (12 servings)

1 teaspoon butter
1 teaspoon white sugar
1 (14 oz.) can sweetened condensed milk
½ cup unsweetened shredded coconut
2 eggs
1 pinch Parmesan cheese, grated

Preparation

At 350 degrees F, preheat your oven. Grease a suitable mini muffin tray with butter and coat with sugar. Next, beat the eggs with cheese, coconut, and milk in a bowl. Pour this mixture in the muffin cups. Place this tray in a roasting pan and add water up to 1 inch in this pan. Bake for 10 minutes and allow the custard cups to cool. Serve.

Brazilian Hash Scramble

Preparation time: 15 minutes
Cook time: 11 minutes
Nutrition facts (per serving): 208 Cal (14g fat, 15g protein, 4g fiber)

The famous Brazilian Hash scramble is essential to try on the Brazilian breakfast menu. Cook at home with these healthy ingredients and enjoy.

Ingredients (5 servings)
5 large eggs
Salt and black pepper, to taste
5 garlic cloves, minced
1 bunch collard greens, chopped
1 large white onion, sliced
1-pound chicken sausages, sliced
1 (15-oz.) can pinto beans, rinsed and drained
2 bay leaves
1 handful parsley and green onions, chopped, for garnish
Olive oil, for cooking

Preparation
Beat the eggs with black pepper and salt in a bowl. Set a skillet over medium heat and grease it with the olive oil. Pour in the eggs and cook for 3 minutes while scrambling it. Sauté 3 minced garlic cloves with a dash of oil in another skillet for 30 seconds and then add the black pepper, salt, and collard greens. Cook for 3 minutes and then transfer to a bowl. Sauté the onion with a dash of oil for 2 minutes until soft. Stir in the remaining garlic and sauté for 30 seconds. Stir in the bay leaves and the beans. Next, cook for 1 minute. Add the scrambled eggs and collard greens. Serve warm.

Brazilian Garlic Cheese Bread (Pao De Queijo)

Preparation time: 10 minutes
Cook time: 20 minutes
Nutrition facts (per serving): 385 Cal (22g fat, 6.3g protein, 0g fiber)

The Brazilian garlic cheese bread is great to serve with all types of eggs dishes and bacon. It has these appealing cheesy tastes that go with everything.

Ingredients (6 servings)
½ cup olive oil
⅓ cup of water
⅓ cup of milk
1 teaspoon salt
2 cups tapioca flour
2 teaspoon garlic, minced
⅔ cup of Parmesan cheese, grated
2 eggs, beaten

Preparation
At 375 degrees F, preheat your oven. Mix the milk, salt, water, and olive in a pan and set it over high heat. Stir in the garlic and the tapioca flour and then mix well. Leave this mixture for 15 minutes. Add the egg and the cheese to the tapioca mixture and mix well. Make ¼ cup sized balls from this mixture and place them on a baking sheet. Bake the balls for 20 minutes. Serve.

Morning Rice Pudding

Preparation time: 15 minutes
Cook time: 2 hours 30 minutes
Nutrition facts (per serving): 570 Cal (46g fat, 12g protein, 2g fiber)

The Brazilian rice pudding is a morning meal that you must serve at the breakfast table. This recipe will add a lot of flavors and aromas to your menu.

Ingredients (2 servings)
¾ cup of dry arborio rice
a pinch of salt
2 cups coconut milk
2 cups whole milk
1 cinnamon stick
2 tablespoons of light brown sugar
½ tablespoon ground cinnamon
2 tablespoon granulated sugar
14 oz. sweetened condensed milk
½ cup warmed hot heavy cream
1 tablespoon pure vanilla extract
4 tablespoons of raisins

Preparation
Add the milk, salt, rice, and cinnamon to a slow cooker and then cook for 2 hours on High heat. Discard the cinnamon stick and add the rest of the ingredients. Cook for 30 minutes on High heat and serve.

Brazilian Bread

Preparation time: 15 minutes
Cook time: 20 minutes
Nutrition facts (per serving): 220 Cal (10.4g fat, 2.4g protein, 18g fiber)

Have you tried the famous Brazilian bread for breakfast? Well, here's a Brazilian delight that adds egg and cheese to your morning meal in a delicious way.

Ingredients (4 servings)
1 large egg
⅓ cup of olive oil
⅔ cup of milk
1 ½ cups of tapioca flour
½ cup cheese, grated
1 teaspoon salt

Preparation
At 400 degrees F, preheat your oven. Grease a suitable mini muffin pan with cooking spray. Blend the egg, tapioca flour, and the rest of the ingredients in a bowl until smooth. Divide this batter in the muffin cups and bake for 20 minutes in the oven. Allow the bread to cool and serve.

Brazilian Passion Fruit Smoothie

Preparation time: 15 minutes
Nutrition facts (per serving): 312 Cal (16g fat, 8g protein, 7g fiber)

The Brazilian fruit smoothie is famous for its delicious flavor and creamy texture. Made from mango, yogurt, honey, and passion fruit juice, this smoothie is a refreshing serving.

Ingredients (1 serving)
1 mango, peeled and diced
½ cup passion fruit juice
½ cup coconut water
¼ cup plain Greek yogurt
1 tablespoon honey
¼ cup ice cubes
Mint sprigs, for garnish

Preparation
Blend the mango with the rest of the ingredients in a blender. Serve chilled.

Brazilian Avocado Smoothie

Preparation time: 10 minutes
Nutrition facts (per serving): 378 Cal (16g fat, 4g protein, 2g fiber)

This Brazilian avocado smoothie tastes heavenly when prepared using the following ingredients. Serve fresh with your favorite egg meal on the side.

Ingredients (2 servings)
2 avocados, peeled and diced
2 cups whole milk, chilled
3 tablespoon sugar
2 teaspoon lime juice

Preparation
Blend the avocado with the rest of the ingredients in a blender. Serve chilled.

Brazilian Sandwich

Preparation time: 15 minutes
Cook time: 22 minutes
Nutrition facts (per serving): 672 Cal (31g fat, 48g protein, 4g fiber)

These sandwiches are a must-have for every fancy dinner. In turn, with the help of this recipe, you can cook them in no time.

Ingredients (4 servings)
1 ½ pounds ground beef
2 garlic cloves, minced
1 tablespoon water
Black pepper, to taste
¼ cup olive oil
2 large sweet onions, sliced
½ teaspoon ground cumin
1 (4 oz.) link linguica sausage, sliced into quarters
4 American cheese, slices
8 deli rye bread slices
2 tablespoon butter, softened
4 teaspoons of Dijon mustard

Preparation
Mix the black pepper, water, garlic, and ground beef in a bowl and then make 4 patties. Place the patties on a sheet, cover, and refrigerate. Sauté the onion and the cumin with oil in medium-high heat for 7 minutes until brown and then transfer to a bowl. Stir in the sausage and cook for 2 minutes per side. Transfer the sausages to a plate. Sear the patties in the same skillet for 5 minutes per side. Then place a cheese slice on top and cook the patties for 2 minutes and transfer to a plate. Grease a bread slice with butter and sear the bread until brown and crispy. Place a patty on top of one bread slice.

Add the onion and the mustard on top and place another bread slice on top. Toast the sandwiches for 2 minutes per side in a skillet.

Baked Eggs

Preparation time: 15 minutes
Cook time: 38 minutes
Nutrition facts (per serving): 256 Cal (16g fat, 31g protein, 6g fiber)

Brazilian baked egg is another nutritious yet simple meal for the breakfast table. It has lots of nutrients and fibers to the table, along with healthy ingredients that are cooked together in a tempting combination.

Ingredients (6 servings)
¼ cup olive oil
3 bell peppers, sliced
1 medium red onion, sliced
2 beefsteak tomatoes, cut into wedges
8 garlic cloves, sliced
1 jalapeño, with seeds, halved
¼ cup fresh basil leaves
2 tablespoon fresh oregano leaves
1½ teaspoon chili powder
1 teaspoon paprika
Salt and black pepper, to taste
1 cup ricotta
6 large eggs
1 cup sharp white cheddar, grated
¼ cup Parmesan, grated
Toasted country-style bread, for serving

Preparation
Sauté the onion and bell peppers with oil in a large pot for 12 minutes. Stir in the paprika, chili powder, oregano, basil, jalapeno, garlic and tomatoes and then cook for 20 minutes. At 400 degrees F,

preheat your oven. Layer a 13 x9 inches baking sheet with cooking spray and spread the bell pepper mixture in it. Make 6 wells from this mixture and add a dollop of ricotta and 1 egg in to the each well. Drizzle the Parmesan, cheddar, black pepper, and salt on top. Bake for 18 minutes in the oven. Serve warm.

Toasted Manioc Flour Meal (Farofa De Ovo E Cebolinha)

Preparation time: 15 minutes
Cook time: 12 minutes
Nutrition facts (per serving): 410 Cal (6g fat, 20g protein, 1.4g fiber)

Try this flour meal for your breakfast, and you'll forget about the rest. The recipe is simple and gives you lots of nutrients in one place.

Ingredients (6 servings)
2 tablespoon unsalted butter
1 ½ cups of manioc flour
2 tablespoon olive oil
4 scallions, sliced
5 large eggs
Salt and black pepper, to taste

Preparation
Set a suitable saucepan over low heat and add butter to melt. Add the flour and toast for 10 minutes with continuous stirring. Keep this flour aside. Set a skillet with oil over medium heat and sauté the scallions for 1 minute. Beat the eggs with black pepper and salt in a bowl. Pour this mixture over the scallions, scramble, and cook until the eggs are set. Add the toasted flour, black pepper, and salt. Serve warm.

Brazilian Dough Balls

Preparation time: 15 minutes
Cook time: 27 minutes
Nutrition facts (per serving): 226 Cal (24g fat, 4g protein, 1g fiber)

The famous Brazilian dough balls reflect one of the Brazilian specialties, so everyone must try this interesting combination of different fillings and unique garnishes.

Ingredients (6 servings)
½ cup whole milk
3 tablespoons of vegetable oil
9 oz. cassava flour
2 large eggs
7 ½ oz. Parmesan cheese, shredded

Preparation
Add the vegetable oil, milk, water, and 1 teaspoon salt to a large pan and cook to a boil. Remove it from the heat, add the flour, and then mix well in a stand mixer until it makes a smooth dough. Beat the eggs, add to the prepared dough, and then mix again for 2 minutes. Stir in the cheese and mix well. Layer a baking sheet with parchment paper. Take 1 tablespoon of the prepared dough and make a small ball. Make more balls in the same way. Place these balls onto the baking sheet and bake for 25 minutes at 400 degrees F.

Brunch Omelet

Preparation time: 15 minutes
Cook time: 10 minutes
Nutrition facts (per serving): 211 Cal (17g fat, 6g protein, 0.7g fiber)

This brunch omelet is the best way to enjoy soft and savory egg meal in the morning in the Brazilian style. Serve with the bread slices.

Ingredients (4 servings)
4 eggs
1 tablespoon butter
1 teaspoon crushed garlic, minced
1-3 oz. Brazilian linguica calabrese, thin sliced
2 tablespoon catupiry cheese, shredded
Ragu, roasted garlic pasta sauce for topping
1 Haas avocado for topping
Hot sauce, as needed

Preparation
Beat the eggs in a bowl and add the calabrese, cheese, and garlic. Set a suitable skillet over medium heat and add the butter to grease. Pour the egg mixture into it and cook for 3-5 minutes per side. Serve warm with avocado and hot sauce on top.

Beans With Fried Bacon And Scrambled Eggs

Preparation time: 10 minutes
Cook time: 18 minutes
Nutrition facts (per serving): 217 Cal (14g fat, 9g protein, 0.3g fiber)

These beans with scrambled egg are a perfect morning meal! You can serve them with your favorite garnishes or preferred toppings.

Ingredients (6 servings)
14 oz. dried beans, soaked in cold water overnight
9 oz. smoked bacon, cubed
5 eggs
2 tablespoon pork lard or vegetable oil
1 onion, chopped
4 garlic cloves, chopped
7 ½ oz. cassava flour
4 oz. torresmo (pork rind), crumbled
2 tablespoons of parsley, chopped
3 tablespoons of spring onion, chopped

Preparation
Add the beans to a pot filled with boiling water and cook until soft then drain. Sauté the bacon in a skillet for 8 minutes until crispy then transfer to a plate. Add the eggs to the same pan, scramble, and cook until set. Transfer the scrambled eggs to a plate. Sauté the onion and the garlic with lard in the same pan for 5 minutes. Stir in the beans and cook for 5 minutes. Add the cassava flour and mix well. Add the torresmo and mix well. Fold the scrambled eggs, bacon, spring onion, and parsley. Serve warm.

Brazilian Cheese Eggs Benedict

Preparation time: 15 minutes
Cook time: 20 minutes
Nutrition facts (per serving): 242 Cal (8g fat, 2g protein, 1g fiber)

If you haven't tried the Brazilian cheese bread eggs before, then here comes a simple and easy to cook meal that you can easily prepare at home with minimum efforts.

Ingredients (14 servings)
Biscuits
14 pieces Brazil Bites dough, thawed
1 tablespoon minced chives
6 tablespoon cheddar cheese shredded

Garnish
4 cups mixed greens
1 basket of cherry tomatoes
8 eggs, poached
1 cup hollandaise sauce

Preparation
At 400 degrees F, preheat your oven. Mix the prepared dough with chives and cheddar and divide into 4 biscuits. Place them on a baking sheet and bake for 20 minutes, flipping them once cooked halfway through. Cut each baked biscuit in half cross sectionally. Place the ham on top of each bottom half of the biscuits. Add the poached eggs and a dollop of hollandaise sauce on top. Garnish with the chives, greens, and tomatoes and place the other half of the biscuits on top. Serve.

Brazilian Savory Pancakes

Preparation time: 10 minutes
Cook time: 11 minutes
Nutrition facts (per serving): 301 Cal (3g fat, 4g protein, 4g fiber)

Do you want to try some pancakes on this menu? Have you ever tried making these pancakes at home? If you haven't, now is the time to cook this delicious meal at home using simple and healthy ingredients.

Ingredients (4 servings)
2 cups flour
2 cups milk
1 teaspoon salt
2 eggs
1 tablespoon oil

Filling
Sliced ham, to taste
Mild cheddar cheese, to taste
1 ½ lbs. tomato sauce

Preparation
Blend the eggs with the milk and the oil in a bowl. Stir in the flour and mix until smooth. Set a pan greased with cooking spray over medium heat. Pour a ladle of this batter into the pan, spread it around, and cook for 2-3 minutes per side. Make more pancakes in the same way. Place the pancakes on a baking sheet, lined with parchment paper. Spread the tomato sauce, cheese, and ham on top of each pancake and broil for 5 minutes. Serve warm.

Brazilian Muffins

Preparation time: 5 minutes
Cook time: 20 minutes
Nutrition facts (per serving): 287 Cal (5g fat, 7.3g protein, 3g fiber)

These muffins are a typical Brazilian side meal, a staple on the Brazilian menu. They're soft, moist, and fluffy.

Ingredients (12 servings)
1 (¼ oz.) envelope of active dry yeast
¼ cup of warm water
6 cups all-purpose flour
1 cup white sugar
3 eggs
¼ cup melted butter cooled
½ teaspoon salt
1 ¼ cups of milk

Preparation
Mix the warm water with the yeast and the sugar in a large suitable bowl and leave it for 10 minutes. Stir in the flour, milk, salt, eggs and then mix until the ingredients come together as a dough. Knead the prepared dough for 10 minutes. Cover the prepared dough with a plastic sheet and leave it for 1 hour. Punch the prepared dough down and cut it into 20 pieces. Spread each dough piece into ½ inch thick round. Place the rounds on a baking sheet lined with parchment paper. Cover them with a kitchen towel and leave it for 1 ½ hour. Add the oil to a suitable deep cooking pan and heat to 350 degrees F. Fry the cakes until golden brown. Transfer to a suitable plate lined with a paper towel. Serve.

Brazilian Acai Bowl

Preparation time: 15 minutes
Nutrition facts (per serving): 87 Cal (5g fat, 1g protein, 5g fiber)

If you haven't tried the creamy Acai bowl before, then here comes a simple and easy-to-follow recipe that you can easily recreate in your kitchen with minimum efforts.

Ingredients (1 serving)
1 banana
1 splash of coconut water
1-2 packets of frozen açai pulp
5 teaspoons of guarana syrup
1 handful of granola
Sliced fruit, to serve

Preparation
Blend the banana with the coconut water, Acai pulp, and guarana syrup in a blender. Pour into a serving bowl and garnish with granola and sliced fruit. Serve.

Acarajé

Preparation time: 15 minutes
Cook time: 6 minutes
Nutrition facts (per serving): 230 Cal (22g fat, 10g protein, 1.4g fiber)

If you haven't tried the Brazilian Acaraje before, then here comes a simple and easy to cook recipe that you can prepare and cook at home with minimum efforts. These are shrimp fritters are stuffed with black eyed peas filling.

Ingredients (6 servings)
16 oz. dry black-eyed peas
2 onions, chopped
Salt, to taste
½ pound shrimp
4 cups coconut milk
1 ½ oz. roasted peanuts
2 ½ oz. cashews
1 cup manioc flour, toasted
Grated ginger, to taste
3 cups dendê oil (palm oil)
Salsa, to serve

Preparation
Soak the peas in water for 8 hours and drain. Blend the peas with the onion in a blender until smooth. Stir in the salt and mix well. Transfer to a bowl. Blend the shrimp with the ginger, manioc flour, onion, cashews, peanuts, and coconut milk in a blender. Add the salt and the palm oil and then mix well. Cook this mixture in a suitable

saucepan over medium heat until it thickens. Add the palm oil to a deep pan and place over medium heat. When the oil gets hot, add a spoon of the shrimp mixture and cook for 2-3 minutes per side. Cook more shrimp cakes from this mixture in the same way. Place the shrimp cakes on a plate, cut a slit in them, and stuff each with the pea mixture and the salsa. Serve.

Shrimp Tapioca Crepes (Tapioca Com Camarão No Dendê)

Preparation time: 15 minutes
Cook time: 10 minutes
Nutrition facts (per serving): 339 Cal (23g fat, 20g protein, 6g fiber)

The classic tapioca crepe with shrimp is here to complete your Brazilian snack menu. This meal can be served and enjoyed on all sorts of celebrations.

Ingredients (4 servings)
Tapioca crepes
⅓ cup of tapioca flour
1 pinch salt
2-3 tablespoon water

Filling
2 tablespoons of vegetable oil
2 tablespoon minced garlic cloves
12 large shrimps raw, shelled and deveined
1 pinch salt
1 pinch black pepper
1 pinch ground cumin
Juice of ½ lime
2 tablespoon palm oil
1 cup mixed salad leaves
¼ cup shredded purple cabbage
4 cherry tomatoes halved
2 tablespoons of chopped cilantro

Preparation

Blend the tapioca flour with salt and water in a bowl until smooth. Set a skillet greased with butter over medium heat. Pour a dollop of flour batter in it, spread around, and cook for 1-2 minutes per side. Cook as many as 4 crepes. Sauté the garlic with the oil in a skillet for 30 seconds. Stir in the shrimp and then sauté for 3 minutes. Add the cumin, black pepper, salt, lime juice, and palm oil. Divide this mixture with the greens, cabbage, and tomatoes in the crepes. Serve.

Brazilian Chicken Croquettes (Coxinha)

Preparation time: 10 minutes
Cook time: 33 minutes
Nutrition facts (per serving): 425 Cal (28g fat, 33g protein, 2g fiber)

Have you tried the Brazilian chicken croquettes before? Well, now you can enjoy this flavorsome meal by using this easy recipe.

Ingredients (6 servings)
1 ½ pounds of boneless chicken breasts
5 cups chicken broth
1 carrot, halved
2 medium onions
2 bay leaves
8 oz. cream cheese, softened
1 lime, juiced
2 garlic cloves
2 tablespoons of butter
Salt, to taste
Pepper, to taste
3 ½ cups all-purpose flour
2 large eggs
3 cups fine breadcrumbs
Vegetable oil, for frying

Preparation
Add the chicken, broth, carrot, onion, and bay leaves to a pan and cook for 20 minutes. Strain and keep the chicken and the broth separately. Shred the chicken and mix with the cream cheese in a bowl. Sauté the onion and the garlic with 2 tablespoons of butter in a

skillet for 5 minutes. Add 3 ½ cups of broth, cook to a boil, add 3 ½ cups flour, and mix well for 3 minutes until it makes a smooth dough. Allow the prepared dough to cool. Take 1 ½ tablespoons of flour dough in your hand, roll into a ball then press over your palm. Add 2 teaspoons of chicken filling at the center and roll the prepared dough again into a ball. Repeat the same steps with the remaining dough and filling. Beat the eggs in one bowl and mix the breadcrumbs with black pepper and salt on a plate. Set a deep pan with oil over medium heat and let it heat to 350 degrees F. Dip each dough ball in the eggs then coat with breadcrumbs and deep fry for 5 minutes until golden brown. Serve.

Grilled Cheese Sticks

Preparation time: 10 minutes
Cook time: 4 minutes
Nutrition facts (per serving): 96 Cal (15g fat, 12g protein, 3g fiber)

Let's have a rich and delicious cheese on the menu. Try them with a sweet chimichurri sauce, and you'll simply love them.

Ingredients (4 servings)
1 (8 oz.) halloumi cheese, sliced
Vegetable oil to brush
Chimichurri sauce molasses, to serve

Preparation
Soak the cheese in cold water for 60 minutes and pat it dry. Set a griddle pan over medium heat. Grease it with cooking spray and grill the cheese for 2 minutes per side. Serve with chimichurri sauce.

Brazilian Pasties With Chicken (Pastel Frito De Frango)

Preparation time: 15 minutes
Cook time: 30 minutes
Nutrition facts (per serving): 289 Cal (13g fat, 3g protein, 2g fiber)

It's about time to try the crispy chicken pasties with some delicious tomato sauce on the side. Now you can also cook them in an air fryer.

Ingredients (3 servings)
3 chicken breasts
1 tablespoon chicken bouillon
2 tablespoon vegetable oil
1 medium onion, minced
3 green onions, chopped
2 teaspoon garlic salt
1 teaspoon oregano
½ teaspoon chili powder
1 tablespoon cornstarch
2 tablespoon tomato paste
4 oz. cream cheese
½ lime, juiced
Salt, to taste
Black pepper, to taste
5 cups of vegetable oil

Pastel dough
3 cups flour
2 tablespoon lard
1 ½ teaspoon salt
½ teaspoon baking powder

1 tablespoon vinegar
1 egg, beaten
¾ cup water
1 tablespoon vodka

Preparation

Add the chicken, bouillon, and water to a suitable saucepan and cook for 5 minutes. Cover and leave this mixture for 10 minutes. Remove the cooked chicken from the hot water and shred it in a bowl. Sauté the green onions and onions with 2 tablespoons of oil in a pan for 5 minutes. Add the cornstarch, chili powder, oregano, and garlic salt and mix well. Stir in the tomato paste and 1 cup of chicken broth and cook until the mixture thickens. Add the shredded chicken and mix well. Remove the chicken from the heat and add the cream cheese. Add the lime juice, black pepper, and salt. Keep this mixture aside. Mix the flour with the egg, vodka, vinegar, baking powder, salt, vegetable shortening, and flour in a bowl. Add a ¾ cup hot water and a ¼ cup of reserved chicken broth. Mix well until it makes a smooth dough. Cover and leave this dough for 10 minutes.

Divide the prepared dough in half and spread each in a ½ inch thick and 9x12 inch rectangle. Cut each rectangle into 10 smaller rectangles and add 2 tablespoons of the chicken mixture over the 10 rectangles. Next, place the remaining rectangles on top. Press the edges to seal them and deep fry these pastries until golden brown. Serve.

Brazilian Quindim

Preparation time: 15 minutes
Cook time: 45 minutes
Nutrition facts (per serving): 279 Cal (5.2g fat, 2.8g protein, 3g fiber)

If you haven't tried the Brazilian Quindim, then you must try them now as they have no parallel in taste and texture.

Ingredients (6 servings)
1 oz. of desiccated coconut
9 oz. of caster sugar
9 oz. of milk
15 egg yolks
1 pinch of salt
½ lemon, juice
1 knob of butter

Preparation
Mix 9 oz. sugar and 5 ½ oz. milk in a pan and cook to a boil. Remove from the heat, stir in the coconut, cover, and leave for 2 hours. Stir in the egg yolks, salt, remaining sugar, milk, and lemon juice. Mix well and set this mixture aside. Grease the dariole molds with butter and dust with sugar. At 300 degrees F, preheat your oven. Divide the coconut mixture in the molds and bake for 45 minutes in the oven. Allow the rounds to cool and serve.

Brazilian Cream Cheese (Requeijão)

Preparation time: 15 minutes
Cook time: 10 minutes
Nutrition facts (per serving): 232 Cal (11g fat, 23g protein, 3g fiber)

This cream cheese is one popular Brazilian delight to serve. It's super quick to make if you have the cheese and milk at home.

Ingredients (8 servings)
4 cups milk
1 cup corn starch
2 cups Parmesan cheese, grated
2 ½ cups mozzarella cheese, shredded
3 tablespoons of butter, unsalted
1 cup of heavy cream
Salt, to taste

Preparation
Mix the milk with the cornstarch in a pot and place over medium-high heat. Stir in the Parmesan, mozzarella, and butter and then cook to a boil. Reduce its heat and cook for 5 minutes. Blend with 1 cup heavy cream in a blender until smooth. Stir in some salt and serve.

Brazilian Beef Pastel

Preparation time: 15 minutes
Cook time: 17 minutes
Nutrition facts (per serving): 246 Cal (23g fat, 12g protein, 3g fiber)

This fried beef pastel is another Brazilian-inspired delight that you should definitely try on this cuisine. Serve with the flavorsome dips.

Ingredients (6 servings)
Pastel Dough
3 cups all-purpose flour
1 tablespoon salt, or to taste
1 cup warm water
1 tablespoon vegetable oil
1 tablespoon white wine vinegar
1 tablespoon cachaça
Vegetable oil, for frying

Beef Filling
2 tablespoons of olive oil
1 small onion, finely chopped
2 garlic cloves, finely minced
½-pound ground beef
Salt and freshly ground pepper, to taste
⅓ cup olives, sliced
⅓ cup of chopped parsley

Preparation
Mix the flour, salt, cachaca, vinegar, oil, and water in a stand mixer until they make a smooth dough. Knead this prepared dough for 5 minutes, cover and leave this dough for 30 minutes. Sauté the garlic and the onion with the oil in a suitable skillet for 2 minutes. Stir in the

beef and cook for 5 minutes. Stir in the parsley, black pepper, salt, and olives. Make ¼ cup sized balls from the prepared dough and spread each ball into a round. Divide the beef on the rounds and fold in half. Press and pinch the edges with a fork to seal the filling. Deep fry the pastels in hot oil until golden brown. Serve.

Hearts Of Palm Pastel

Preparation time: 15 minutes
Cook time: 17 minutes
Nutrition facts (per serving): 146 Cal (21g fat, 9g protein, 4.1g fiber)

These hearts of palm stuffed pastels are everyone's favorite go-to meal when it comes to serving Brazilian meals; you can prepare them in no time.

Ingredients (6 servings)
Pastel Dough
3 cups of all-purpose flour
1 tablespoon of salt, or to taste
1 cup warm water
1 tablespoon of vegetable oil
1 tablespoon of white wine vinegar
1 tablespoon of cachaça
Vegetable oil for frying

Hearts of Palm Filling
1 tablespoon of olive oil
2 tablespoons of butter
1 small onion, chopped
2 garlic cloves, minced
¼ cup flour
1 cup milk
½ cup of tomato sauce
1 (14 oz.) can heart of palm, chopped
⅓ cup of olives, chopped
Salt and black pepper, to taste
¼ cup of parsley, chopped

Preparation

Mix the flour, salt, cachaca, vinegar, oil, and water in a stand mixer until they make a smooth dough. Knead this prepared dough for 5 minutes, cover and leave this dough for 30 minutes. Sauté the onion, garlic, butter, and oil in a skillet until soft. Stir in the hearts of palms and cook for 2 minutes. Add the tomato sauce, the flour and the milk. Cook until the mixture thickens. Fold in the olives, black pepper, salt, and parsley. Make ¼ cup sized balls from the prepared dough and spread each ball into a round. Divide the filling on the rounds and fold in half. Press and pinch the edges with a fork to seal the filling. Deep fry the pastels in hot oil until golden brown. Serve.

Cheese Pastel

Preparation time: 10 minutes
Cook time: 10 minutes
Nutrition facts (per serving): 172 Cal (5g fat, 1.4g protein, 2g fiber)

Brazilian cheese pastels are another great side serving for the table, and you can serve them as a delicious and healthy snack meal as well.

Ingredients (6 servings)
Pastel Dough
3 cups all-purpose flour
1 tablespoon salt, or to taste
1 cup warm water
1 tablespoon vegetable oil
1 tablespoon white wine vinegar
1 tablespoon cachaça
Vegetable oil, for frying

Cheese Filling
8 oz. cheese, sliced

Preparation
Mix the flour, salt, cachaca, vinegar, oil and water in a stand mixer until they make a smooth dough. Knead this prepared dough for 5 minutes, cover, and leave this dough for 30 minutes. Shred cheese and keep it aside. Make ¼ cup sized balls from the prepared dough and spread each ball into a round. Divide the cheese on the rounds and fold in half. Press and pinch the edges with a fork to seal the filling. Deep fry the pastels in hot oil until golden brown. Serve.

Brazilian Chicken Wings

Preparation time: 10 minutes
Cook time: 7 minutes
Nutrition facts (per serving): 102 Cal (5g fat, 5g protein, 2g fiber)

These chicken wings are another popular appetizer in the Brazilian Cuisine. It delivers this great taste from the mix of garlic and lime juice.

Ingredients (6 servings)
2 lbs. small chicken wings
Juice of 3 limes
5 garlic cloves, minced
5 garlic cloves, sliced
¼ cup olive oil
½ cup flour
Red pepper flakes, to taste
Salt and black pepper, to taste
Vegetable oil, to fry

Preparation
Toss the chicken wings with the garlic, black pepper, salt, and lime juice in a bowl. Cover and refrigerate overnight. Dredge the marinated wings through the flour to coat. Deep fry these coated chicken wings in hot oil for 5-7 minutes until golden brown. Drizzle the red pepper, black pepper, and salt over the chicken wings. Serve.

Salads

Gaucho Potato Salad

Preparation time: 15 minutes
Cook time: 5 minutes
Nutrition facts (per serving): 160 Cal (15g fat, 1g protein, 2g fiber)

The Brazilian gaucho potato salad is famous for its texture, taste, and aroma, and now you can bring those unique flavors home by using this simple recipe.

Ingredients (4 servings)
1 lb. new potatoes, peeled, diced and boiled
1 tablespoon of olive oil
2 teaspoons of fresh mint, chopped
2 cobs of sweetcorn, boiled
3 ½ oz. peas
1 carrot, peeled and diced
1 apple, peeled and diced
2 shallots, sliced
2 tablespoons of mayonnaise
Juice of half a lemon

Preparation
Sauté the potatoes with the oil in a skillet for 5 minutes and transfer to a bowl. Stir in the rest of the ingredients. Mix well and serve.

Brazilian Seafood Salad

Preparation time: 10 minutes
Nutrition facts (per serving): 211 Cal (20g fat, 4g protein, 13g fiber)

This seafood salad is the right fit to serve with all your Brazilian entrees. Here the salad leaves, mango, and beans are mixed to make an amazing combination.

Ingredients (4 servings)
1 oz. mixed salad leaves
5 oz. sweetcorn
1 small mango, peeled, and diced
14 oz. tin black beans, drained and rinsed
5 oz. cooked squid rings
5 oz. king prawns, cooked and peeled
1 lime, cut into wedges

Chimichurri Dressing
2 onions, chopped
1 bunch flat-leaf parsley, chopped
1 teaspoon fresh oregano leaves, chopped
1 small bunch coriander, chopped
1 garlic clove, chopped
2 tablespoons of olive oil
1 lime, zest and juice

Preparation
Blend all the chimichurri ingredients in a blender. Toss the prawns with the rest of the salad ingredients in a salad bowl. Pour the chimichurri dressing on top. Serve.

Colorful Avocado Salad

Preparation time: 10 minutes
Nutrition facts (per serving): 176 Cal (13g fat, 3g protein, 4g fiber)

This avocado salad is a delicious and healthy salad, which has a refreshing taste due to the use of herbs and spices. It's great to serve with skewers.

Ingredients (4 servings)
1 medium tomato, cut into eighths
½ small cucumber, thinly sliced
1 small red onion, sliced
⅓ cup of julienned green pepper
2 tablespoons of Italian salad dressing
1 medium ripe avocado, peeled and cubed

Preparation
Toss the cucumber with the onion and the rest of the ingredients in a salad bowl. Serve.

Brazilian Potato Salad

Preparation time: 10 minutes
Nutrition facts (per serving): 179 Cal (16g fat, 15g protein, 3g fiber)

The Brazilian Potato salad is a special creamy salad, and it's special to serve with all the different entrees. Use this quick and simple recipe to get it ready in no time.

Ingredients (4 servings)
2 ½ pounds potatoes, peeled, cubed, boiled
1 pinch salt, plus enough to taste
1 tablespoon of apple cider vinegar
1 cup of mayonnaise
4 tablespoons of lime juice
1 garlic clove, minced
¼ large white onion, grated
½ cup olives, chopped
2 tablespoons of fresh mint, chopped
3 tablespoons of cilantro, chopped
3 tablespoons of green onions, chopped
Black pepper to taste
2 large hard-boiled eggs, chopped

Preparation
Mix the potatoes with the eggs and the rest of the ingredients in a bowl. Serve.

Brazilian Kale Salad

Preparation time: 10 minutes
Nutrition facts (per serving): 276 Cal (17g fat, 7g protein, 3g fiber)

It's almost if the Brazilian menu is incomplete without this kale salad. Made with kale, cabbage, and carrots, it adds lots of nutritional value to your life here.

Ingredients (4 servings)
2 x 7 ½ oz. packs curly kale, sliced
¼ small red cabbage, shredded
2 carrots, peeled and julienned
1 avocado, sliced
7 ½ oz. cherry tomatoes, halved
4 tablespoons of extra-virgin olive oil
½ orange, juiced
2 tablespoons of red wine vinegar

Preparation
Toss the kales with the rest of the ingredients in a salad bowl. Serve.

Brazilian Chicken Salad (Salpicão De Frango)

Preparation time: 10 minutes
Nutrition facts (per serving): 155 Cal (8g fat, 3g protein, 2g fiber)

If you haven't tried this chicken salad before, then here comes a simple and easy to cook recipe that you can easily recreate in your kitchen with minimum efforts.

Ingredients (4 servings)
1 ½ lbs. chicken breasts, boneless, skinless
1 tablespoon of Brazilian Sofrito or 3 garlic cloves minced and ½ onion diced
1 cup of shredded carrots
½ cup of green onions sliced
1 cup of yellow corn
½ cup of raisins
½ cup of mayonnaise
¼ cup of olive oil
¼ cup of white wine vinegar
1 tablespoon of mustard

Preparation
Season the chicken liberally with black pepper and salt and sear with oil for 5 -10 minutes per side. Shred the cooked chicken and for now keep it aside. Mix the carrots and the rest of the ingredients in a salad bowl. Fold in the shredded chicken and mix well. Serve.

Brazilian Onion Salad

Preparation time: 10 minutes
Nutrition facts (per serving): 243 Cal (13g fat, 5g protein, 2g fiber)

Brazilian onion salad is that one recipe that everyone must try on this menu. It contains basic ingredients like tomatoes and onions.

Ingredients (4 servings)
2 large white onions, sliced
2 green onions, chopped
10 cherry tomatoes, quartered
2 tablespoons of olive oil
1 tablespoon of red wine vinegar
½ teaspoon of salt
¼ teaspoon of black pepper

Preparation
Toss the onions with the rest of the ingredients in a bowl. Serve.

Brazilian Hearts Of Palm Salad

Preparation time: 15 minutes
Nutrition facts (per serving): 381 Cal (5g fat, 3g protein, 6g fiber)

If you haven't tried this heart of palm salad before, then here comes a simple and easy to make salad recipe that you can easily recreate in your kitchen with minimum efforts.

Ingredients (4 servings)
2 (14 oz.) cans of hearts of palm, drained and sliced
1 medium tomato, chopped
½ of a small onion, sliced
2 spring onions, chopped
3 tablespoons of olive oil
2 teaspoons of fresh lime juice
¼ teaspoon salt
1 pinch of black pepper

Preparation
Mix the hearts of palm with the rest of the ingredients in a salad bowl. Serve.

Brazilian Tomato Slaw

Preparation time: 15 minutes
Nutrition facts (per serving): 93 Cal (7g fat, 1.4g protein, 4g fiber)

The Brazilian tomato slaw is a delight to serve with all entrees. It's famous for its comforting effects, and the meal offers a very energizing combination of ingredients.

Ingredients (8 servings)
5 tomatoes, diced
½ English cucumber, quartered and sliced
1 red bell pepper, seeded and diced
½ cup onion, diced
½ cup fresh parsley, chopped
¼ cup lime juice
¼ cup olive oil
¼ cup green onions, diced
¼ cup fresh cilantro, chopped
2 tablespoons of cider vinegar
Salt and black pepper to taste

Preparation
Toss the tomatoes with the rest of the ingredients in a salad bowl. Serve.

Brazilian Chopped Salad

Preparation time: 10 minutes
Nutrition facts (per serving): 260 Cal (3g fat, 3g protein, 11g fiber)

Try this Brazilian chopped salad with your favorite herbs on top. Adding a dollop of cream or yogurt will make it even richer in taste.

Ingredients (4 servings)
14 oz. hearts of palm
12 oz. cherry or grape tomatoes
1 fennel bulb, chopped
1 ripe avocado, chopped
½ small red onion, chopped
¼ cup of mint, chopped
Lime Vinaigrette
¼ cup lime juice
¼ cup olive oil
1 garlic clove, minced
1 teaspoon of honey
Salt and black pepper, to taste

Preparation
Toss the hearts of palm with the rest of the ingredients in a salad bowl. Serve.

Black-Eyed Peas Tuna Salad

Preparation time: 10 minutes
Nutrition facts (per serving): 72 Cal (5g fat, 1.4g protein, 2g fiber)

The black-eyed peas tuna salad makes a superb side serving for the table, and you can serve as a delicious and healthy snack meal as well.

Ingredients (6 servings)
1 ½ cup black-eyed peas, boiled
5 tablespoons of olive oil
3 tablespoons of white wine vinegar
1 small yellow onion, sliced
2 small garlic cloves, minced
4 tablespoons of parsley leaves, sliced
9 oz. canned tuna in oil, drained and flaked
Salt and black pepper, to taste

Preparation
Add the black-eyed peas, olive oil, wine vinegar, onion, garlic, parsley, tuna, salt, and black pepper to a salad bowl. Mix well and serve.

Tuna Salad

Preparation time: 10 minutes
Cook time: 20 minutes
Nutrition facts (per serving): 56 Cal (3.5g fat, 5.7g protein, 2g fiber)

This tuna salad is another most popular salad in Brazilian cuisine, and it has this great taste that from the mix of chickpeas and olives.

Ingredients (4 servings)
1 (15-oz.) can chickpeas, drained
1 ½ lb. potatoes, cut into pieces
4 hard-boiled eggs, quartered
½ red onion, diced
⅓ cup of Kalamata olives in oil, drained
12 oz. canned tuna
2 tablespoons of olive oil
2 tablespoons of red wine vinegar
Sea salt, to taste
Black pepper, to taste

Preparation
Boil the salted water in a large suitable pot and add the potatoes. Cook until the potatoes are soft, then drain, then transfer to a bowl. Stir in the chickpeas, onion, olives, tuna, olive oil, vinegar, black pepper, salt, and eggs. Mix well and serve.

Brazilian Shrimp Soup

Preparation time: 10 minutes
Cook time: 25 minutes
Nutrition facts (per serving): 361 Cal (14g fat, 2g protein, 2g fiber)

Enjoy this Brazilian shrimp soup recipe with rice. Adding cream or sour cream on top offers a very nice taste to the soup.

Ingredients (4 servings)
2 tablespoons of cooking oil
1 onion, chopped
1 green bell pepper, chopped
3 garlic cloves, minced
¾ cup long-grain rice
¼ teaspoon of red-pepper flakes
1 ¾ teaspoon of salt
1 ¾ cups of canned crushed tomatoes
5 cups of water
1 cup of canned unsweetened coconut milk
1 ½ pounds of medium shrimp, shelled
¼ teaspoon of black pepper
1 tablespoon of lemon juice
½ cup of fresh parsley, chopped

Preparation
Sauté the garlic, bell pepper, and onion with oil in a large pot for 10 minutes. Stir in the water, tomatoes, salt, red pepper flakes, and rice. Next, cook for 10 minutes. Add the coconut milk and cook to a simmer. Add the shrimp and cook for 5 minutes. Adjust the seasoning with parsley, lemon juice, and black pepper. Serve warm.

Brazilian Black Bean Soup

Preparation time: 10 minutes
Cook time: 4 hours
Nutrition facts (per serving): 180 Cal (4g fat, 15g protein, 3g fiber)

This black bean soup is everything I was looking for. The black beans, tomatoes, and carrots in this soup make a complete package for a health enthusiast like me.

Ingredients (6 servings)
2 jalapeño peppers, chopped
2 tablespoons of olive oil
3 cups of onion, chopped
1 ½ cups of carrot, diced
5 garlic cloves, minced
4 cups of vegetable broth
4 (15 oz.) cans of black beans, rinsed
1 (28 oz.) can of fire-roasted diced tomatoes
3 tablespoons of molasses
2 tablespoons of lime zest
5 tablespoons of lime juice
1 ½ teaspoon of ground cumin
1 ½ teaspoon of smoked paprika
⅛ teaspoon of cayenne pepper, or to taste
3 bay leaves
1 teaspoon of salt
¾ teaspoon of black pepper
4 cups o kale, chopped
Chopped scallions, for garnish
Chopped fresh tomato, for garnish

Preparation

Add the beans and the rest of the ingredient to a slow cooker. Cover and cook for 4 hours on High heat. Serve warm.

Brazilian Chicken And Rice Soup

Preparation time: 15 minutes
Cook time: 42 minutes
Nutrition facts (per serving): 270 Cal (16g fat, 16g protein, 5g fiber)

You won't know until you try it! That's what people told me about this chicken and rice soup, and it indeed tasted more unique and flavorsome than other chicken soups I've tried.

Ingredients (6 servings)
2 tablespoons of olive oil
1 onion, chopped
2 garlic cloves, minced
2 lbs. chicken breast
8 cups of water
2 bouillon cubes
2 potatoes, peeled and diced
Salt and black pepper to taste
2 tomatoes, quartered
2 celery sticks, halved
2 carrots, peeled and diced
2 cups of cooked rice

Garnish
Chopped parsley, to taste

Preparation
Sauté the garlic and onions with oil in a deep pan for 2 minutes. Season the chicken with black pepper and salt and place in the pan. Add the tomatoes, celery sticks and enough water to cover. Put on its lid and cook for 20 minutes. Remove the chicken from the broth, strain this broth, and keep the broth aside. Discard the veggies.

Shred the cooked chicken and remove or discard the bones. Add the broth, chicken, carrots, bouillon and potatoes to a suitable saucepan. Cover and cook for 15 minutes. Stir in the rice and cook for 5 minutes. Add the parsley, black pepper, and salt. Serve warm.

Brazilian Lentil Soup With Kale

Preparation time: 15 minutes
Cook time: 45 minutes
Nutrition facts (per serving): 295 Cal (17g fat, 28g protein, 3g fiber)

If you haven't tried this lentil soup with kale before, then here comes a simple and easy cook recipe that you can easily recreate in your kitchen with minimum efforts.

Ingredients (6 servings)
1 tablespoon of olive oil
1 onion, diced
2 carrots, diced
1 celery stalk, diced
3 garlic cloves, chopped
5 cups of chicken stock
1 tomato, diced
1 cup of lentils, rinsed
1 bay leaf
1 cup of kale, chopped
Salt and black pepper, to taste

Preparation
Sauté the onions with oil in a deep pan for 3 minutes. Add the carrots, garlic, and celery for 5 minutes. Stir in the bay leaf, lentils, diced tomato, and chicken stock. Cook to a simmer, cover and cook for 35 minutes. Add the kale and cook for 2 minutes. Discard the bay leaf and serve warm.

Brazilian Turkey Soup

Preparation time: 15 minutes
Cook time: 35 minutes
Nutrition facts (per serving): 312 Cal (10g fat, 21g protein, 4g fiber)

You can give this turkey soup a try because it has a good and delicious combination of turkey meat, tomatoes, and peanuts.

Ingredients (6 servings)
1 teaspoon of canola oil
½ cup of onion, chopped
3 garlic cloves, minced
1 medium jalapeño chile pepper, chopped
1 tablespoon of fresh ginger, minced
1 (28 oz.) can of fire-roasted tomatoes, diced
1 12-oz. bottle of light beer or non-alcoholic beer
1 cup of chicken broth
¼ cup of unsalted dry roasted peanuts
3 cups of shredded cooked turkey breast
½ cup of unsweetened light coconut milk
½ cup of snipped fresh cilantro
⅓ cup of snipped fresh parsley
1 tablespoon of lime juice
½ teaspoon of black pepper
¼ teaspoon of salt
Snipped, fresh cilantro

Preparation
Sauté the garlic and onion with oil in a deep pan for 2 minutes. Stir in the ginger and the jalapeno pepper and cook for 30 seconds. Stir in the broth, beer, and tomatoes and cook for 20 minutes on a simmer. Meanwhile, grind the peanuts in a food processor and mix

with the coconut milk and the turkey in a bowl. Add this peanut mixture to the tomatoes and cook for 5 minutes with occasional stirring. Stir in the salt, black pepper, lime juice, parsley, and cilantro. Cook for 5 minutes. Serve warm.

Feijoada Soup

Preparation time: 15 minutes
Cook time: 5 hours 5 minutes
Nutrition facts (per serving): 314 Cal (6g fat, 20g protein, 2g fiber)

This Feijoada soup is loved by all, young and adult. It's simple and quick to make. This delight is perfect to serve at dinner tables. It's made with beans and kielbasa sausages.

Ingredients (4 servings)
2 lbs. of dried black beans
1 tablespoon of vegetable oil
4 cups of onions, chopped
¾ lb. of turkey Polish kielbasa, diced
4 garlic cloves, minced
2 teaspoons of cumin, ground
6 cups of water
1 teaspoon of salt
¼ teaspoon of pepper
1 of bay leaf
½ cup of red wine vinegar
½ teaspoon of hot sauce

Preparation
Add the beans and enough water to cover to a deep pan and soak for 4 hours. Drain and keep them aside. Sauté the garlic, onion, and kielbasa with oil in a skillet for 10 minutes. Stir in the cumin and cook for almost 1 minute. Add the water, the rest of the ingredients, and then cook for 1 hour. Discard the bay leaf and serve warm.

Brazilian Sausage Kale Soup

Preparation time: 15 minutes
Cook time: 65 minutes
Nutrition facts (per serving): 565 Cal (26g fat, 25g protein, 4g fiber)

If you haven't tried the classic sausage kale soup before, then here comes an authentic, simple, and easy to cook recipe that you can recreate easily at home in minimum time.

Ingredients (6 servings)
12 oz. of linguica sausage, sliced
1 tablespoon of olive oil
1 onion, diced
1 pinch of salt
3 pounds of russet potatoes, peeled and sliced
2 teaspoon of salt
2 quarts of chicken broth
2 pounds of kale, chopped
1 pinch of cayenne pepper

Preparation
Sauté the sausage with oil in a pot over medium-high heat for 5 minutes until brown. Transfer the sausage to a plate and add the onion and a pinch of salt to the same pot. Next, cook for 5 minutes. Stir in the potatoes, 2 teaspoons of salt, and chicken broth. Cook on a simmer for 10 minutes. Once soft, lightly mash the potatoes with a fork. Stir in the kale and the sausage and cook on a simmer for 45 minutes.

Tomato Soup With Eggs

Preparation time: 15 minutes
Cook time: 1 hour 32 minutes
Nutrition facts (per serving): 358 Cal (14g fat, 9g protein, 4g fiber)

You can give this tomato soup a try because it has a good and delicious combination of tomatoes with poached eggs.

Ingredients (6 servings)
4 bacon slices, cut into pieces
¼ lb. cured Brazilian chorizo sausage, sliced
6 garlic cloves, minced
2 (28-oz.) cans of whole peeled tomatoes, crushed
Salt and black pepper, to taste
6 eggs
6 Brazilian Pão slices (cheese bread), lightly toasted

Preparation
Sauté the bacon in a 6 qt. saucepan for 10 minutes and then transfer to a plate. Add the sausage to the same pan and sauté for 5 minutes. Transfer the sausage to a plate. Add the onions to the same pan and sauté for 10 minutes. Add the garlic and sauté for 2 minutes. Add 2 cups water, black pepper, salt, and tomatoes and then cook on medium-low heat for 1 hour. Puree the hot tomato soup in a blender and then return to the pan. Crack one egg into the soup at a time and cook for 5 minutes. Serve warm with bread.

Chicken Noodle Soup

Preparation time: 5 minutes
Cook time: 35 minutes
Nutrition facts (per serving): 159 Cal (7.1g fat, 17g protein, 1.8g fiber)

A perfect mix of chicken and noodles is all that you need to expand your Brazilian menu. Simple and easy to make, this recipe is a must to try.

Ingredients (6 servings)
1 bone-in chicken breast
1 onion, cut into wedges
4 sprigs of fresh parsley
½ teaspoon of lemon zest
1 sprig of fresh mint
6 cups of chicken stock
⅓ cup of thin egg noodles
2 tablespoons of fresh mint leaves, chopped
Salt, to taste
¼ teaspoon of white pepper

Preparation
Add the mint sprig, lemon zest, parsley, onion, chicken bread, and stock to a suitable saucepan. Cook for 35 minutes and then remove the chicken from the pot. Slice the chicken into pieces. Strain the remaining broth and add to a suitable saucepan. Add the chopped mint, pasta, white pepper, and salt. Cook until the pasta is soft. Stir in the chicken slices and the lemon juice. Garnish with lemon slices and mint leaf. Serve warm.

Green Cabbage Soup

Preparation time: 15 minutes
Cook time: 26 minutes
Nutrition facts (per serving): 456 Cal (27g fat, 11g protein, 4g fiber)

Do you want to enjoy a cabbage stew with a Brazilian twist? Then try this Brazilian cabbage Caldo Verde recipe. You can serve it with your bread.

Ingredients (6 servings)
3 tablespoons of olive oil
1 onion, chopped
3 garlic cloves, crushed
6 potatoes, peeled and sliced
1-pound of cabbage, sliced
2 quarts of water
8 oz. of Brazilian chorizo sausage, sliced
1 of teaspoon smoked paprika
2 teaspoons of salt
Black pepper, to taste
Olive oil

Preparation
Sauté the garlic and the onion with 3 tablespoons of oil in a Dutch oven for 3 minutes. Stir in half of the cabbage and sliced potatoes and then sauté for 3 minutes. Add water and cook the mixture to a boil. Reduce the heat, cover, and cook for 15 minutes on a simmer. Puree the soup until smooth. Stir in the black pepper, salt, paprika, remaining cabbage, and sausage, cover, and cook on a simmer for 5 minutes. Serve warm with some olive oil on top.

Sausage Kidney Bean Soup

Preparation time: 15 minutes
Cook time: 2 hours 40 minutes
Nutrition facts (per serving): 68 Cal (13g fat, 13.3g protein, 3g fiber)

This Brazilian kidney bean soup is an entrée that you must serve during a festive celebration. This recipe will add a lot of appeal and color to your dinner table.

Ingredients (6 servings)
1 ham hock
1 (10 oz.) of linguica sausage, sliced
1 onion, minced
2 quarts of water
4 potatoes, peeled and cubed
2 celery rib, chopped
2 carrots, chopped
1 (15 oz.) can of stewed tomatoes
1 (8 oz.) can of tomato sauce
1 garlic clove, minced
½ head cabbage, sliced
1 (15 oz.) can of kidney beans

Preparation
Add the water, onion, linguica, and ham hock to a Dutch oven and place it over high heat. Cook the mixture to a boil and then reduce the heat. Cover and cook on a simmer for 1 hour. Remove the meat from the pot, chop it, and then return to the pot. Add the garlic, tomato sauce, tomatoes, carrots, celery, and potatoes, cover, and cook for 1 ½ hour on a simmer. Add kidney beans and cabbage and then cook for 10 minutes. Serve warm.

Kale And Cabbage Soup

Preparation time: 10 minutes
Cook time: 65 minutes
Nutrition facts (per serving): 199 Cal (7.9g fat, 11g protein, 2.4g fiber)

Brazilian Kale and cabbage soup is here to make your meal special. You can always serve the soup with your favorite side meal.

Ingredients (8 servings)
4 tomatoes, peeled and chopped
1 tablespoon of butter
1 tablespoon of dried minced onion
Salt and black pepper, to taste
2 tablespoons of olive oil
4 celery stalks, chopped
1 onion, chopped
3 garlic cloves, minced
2 bay leaves
8 cups of hot water
½ head green cabbage, shredded
½ cup of beef base
1 teaspoon of Herbes de Provence
1 pinch of red pepper flakes
1 (15 oz.) can of kidney beans, drained
1 bunch of kale, chopped

Preparation
Add the black pepper, salt, onion, butter, and tomatoes to a suitable saucepan and cook over medium heat for 15 minutes. Sauté the onion, bay leaves, and garlic with olive oil in a stockpot for 5 minutes over medium heat. Stir in the cooked tomato mixture and cook for 5 minutes. Discard the bay leaves and add the water, green cabbage,

red pepper flakes, Herbes de Provence, and beef base. Cover partially and cook for 25 minutes. Add the kale and kidney beans and cover again to cook for 15 minutes. Serve warm.

Fish Soup

Preparation time: 15 minutes
Cook time: 21 minutes
Nutrition facts (per serving): 153 Cal (31g fat, 101g protein, 2g fiber)

This fish soup tastes amazing, and it simple and easy to cook. It's heavenly for all seafood lovers and can be best served in winters.

Ingredients (6 servings)
4 boneless shark fish chunks
1 bunch fresh oregano
1 bay leaf
Rustic bread, sliced
Sweet paprika, to taste
Salt, to taste
4 garlic cloves, sliced
¼ cup of white wine vinegar
1 of tablespoon plain flour
½ cup of olive oil
2 cups of water
Black pepper, to taste
1 egg, beaten
1 onion, chopped
½ green pepper, chopped
1 tablespoon of tomato paste
1 fish stock cube

Preparation
Mix ½ teaspoon paprika, bay leaf, 3 tablespoon olive oil and vinegar in a suitable bowl and the fish pieces. Mix well, cover, and marinate for almost 2 hours. Sauté the onion, green pepper, and garlic with olive oil in a pan for 6 minutes. Stir in the water, fish with its

marinade, stock cube, salt, black pepper, and tomato paste. Discard the bay leaf and cover the lid to cook for 10 minutes. Add 1 ½ tablespoon flour, mix, and cook until the soup thickens. Stir in the egg and cook for 5 minutes. Garnish with thyme. Serve warm.

Macaroni Bean Soup

Preparation time: 15 minutes
Cook time: 2 hours 10 minutes
Nutrition facts (per serving): 573 Cal (31g fat, 29g protein, 7g fiber)

A perfect mix of Brazilian sausages, cabbage, macaroni, beans, and ham, this soup recipe is a warming bliss for all. Serve warm with your favorite bread.

Ingredients (6 servings)
2 pounds of spicy Brazilian sausage, sliced
1-pound of ham hocks
1 onion, sliced
2 quarts water
2 carrots, diced
3 potatoes, diced
1 small head cabbage, chopped
1 (8 oz.) can of tomato sauce
2 (15 oz.) cans of kidney beans
1 (16 oz.) package of macaroni

Preparation
Add the water, onion, ham hocks, and sausage to a large pot, cover, and cook for 1 hour on a simmer. Then remove the ham from the soup and cut it into pieces. Return the ham hock to the pot. Add the tomato sauce, cabbage, potatoes, and carrots, cover, and cook for 60 minutes. Add the pasta and beans and then cook for 10 minutes. Serve warm.

Chicken Soup (Canja De Galinha)

Preparation time: 15 minutes
Cook time: 25 minutes
Nutrition facts (per serving): 138 Cal (6g fat, 4g protein, 1.2g fiber)

The Brazilian chicken soup is here to complete your Brazilian menu. This meal can be served and enjoyed on all sorts of celebrations.

Ingredients (12 servings)
2 tablespoons of olive oil
1 medium yellow onion small diced
2 garlic cloves minced
10-½-oz. de-boned chicken breast, cubed
¾ cup raw long-grain rice rinsed
2 tablespoons of dry white wine
10 cups of chicken broth
¾ cup of potato, peeled and cubed
¾ cup of carrot peeled and cubed
¾ cup of peas
Salt and white pepper, to taste
1 teaspoon of dried thyme
1 bay leaf
6 eggs
¼ cup of parsley chopped
Shredded Parmesan cheese, to sprinkle

Preparation
Sauté the onion with 2 tablespoon oil in a medium pot for almost 30 seconds. Stir in the chicken and cook for 3 minutes. Add the rice and the wine and cook for 1 minute. Add the vegetables, chicken stock, bay leaf, thyme, black pepper and salt and then cook to a boil. Cover, reduce the heat, and cook for 12 minutes. Stir in the eggs

and cook for 8 minutes on a simmer. Discard the bay leaf and garnish with oil and cheese. Serve warm.

Brazilian Fish Stew (Moqueca)

Preparation time: 10 minutes
Cook time: 30 minutes
Nutrition facts (per serving): 310 Cal (11g fat, 22g protein, 6g fiber)

Make this Brazilian fish stew in no time and enjoy it with some garnish on top. Adding a drizzle of paprika on top makes it super tasty.

Ingredients (6 servings)
Fish
1 ½ pounds Halibut
½ teaspoon salt
1 lime, zest and juice

Stew
3 tablespoons of coconut oil
1 onion, finely diced
½ teaspoon salt
1 cup carrot, diced
1 red bell pepper, diced
4 garlic cloves, chopped
½ jalapeno, diced
1 tablespoon of tomato paste
2 teaspoons of paprika
1 teaspoon of ground cumin
1 cup of fish stock
1 ½ cups of tomatoes, diced
1 (14 oz.) can of coconut milk

Salt, to taste
½ cup of cilantro, chopped

Preparation
Season the fish with the lime juice, zest, and salt in a bowl. Sauté the onion with salt and oil in a deep pan for 3 minutes. Stir in the jalapeno, garlic, bell pepper, and carrot and sauté for 5 minutes. Stir in the stock, spices, and tomato paste and cook to a simmer. Cover and cook for 5 minutes. Add the coconut milk and cook for 6 minutes. Place the fish in the pan and cook for 5-10 minutes until done. Garnish with the cilantro and scallions. Serve warm.

Chicken Fricassee With Shoestring Potatoes

Preparation time: 5 minutes
Cook time: 34 minutes
Nutrition facts (per serving): 204 Cal (9g fat, 6g protein, 1.7g fiber)

Try the chicken fricassees with potatoes at the dinner as the meal is infused with an amazing blend of chicken, olives, and cream. Serve warm with your favorite bread.

Ingredients (6 servings)
2 ¼ lbs. chicken thighs
1 cup of heavy whipping cream
1 can of whole corn kernel drained
1 (8 oz.) package of cream cheese, softened
¾ sliced green olives
Salt and black pepper, to taste
2 cups of mozzarella cheese, shredded
Store-bought shoestring potatoes

Preparation
At 350 degrees F, preheat your oven. Add the chicken, black pepper, salt, and chicken stock to a suitable saucepan and cook until chicken is soft. Shred the cooked chicken and for now keep it aside. Blend the heavy cream with cream cheese and corn in a blender until creamy. Stir this mixture with chicken, olives, black pepper, and salt in a pan. Cook for 4 minutes. Spread the chicken mixture in a greased casserole dish and drizzle with shredded cheese on top. Bake for 20 minutes and then spread potatoes on top. Serve warm.

Cod In Cheese Sauce (Bacalao Quatro Queijos)

Preparation time: 10 minutes
Cook time: 20 minutes
Nutrition facts (per serving): 102 Cal (3g fat, 11g protein, 2g fiber)

This cod soaked in cheese sauce is a typical Brazilian entree, which is a must on the Brazilian menu. It has this rich mix of buttery milk and cheese sauce.

Ingredients (6 servings)
6 cod fillets, ½-inch thick
Salt, to taste
1 pinch black pepper
1 pinch paprika
5 tablespoons of grapeseed oil
4 tablespoons of unsalted butter
4 ½ tablespoons of all-purpose flour
3 cups of warmed milk
1 pinch of ground nutmeg
2 ½ cups blend of shredded cheeses
6 cherry tomatoes, halved
8 olives, sliced
½ jalapeno, sliced
Parsley or chives, chopped

Preparation
Soak the cod in a pan filled with water for 24 hours and remove from the heat. Debone and remove the skin from the fillets. Pat dry the cod fillets with paper towel. Season them with paprika, black pepper, and salt. Sear the cod in a skillet greased with 3 tablespoons of oil, for 3 minutes per side. Keep this fish aside. Add the butter to a

suitable pan and melt it. Stir in the flour and cook for almost 1 minute with stirring. Pour in the milk, mix well, and cook for 7 minutes until it thickens. Add the nutmeg, black pepper, and salt. Stir in 2 cups of cheeses and mix well. Place the fish in this pan and broil for 5 minutes in the oven. Serve warm.

Picanha Roast

Preparation time: 5 minutes
Cook time: 70 minutes
Nutrition facts (per serving): 320 Cal (32g fat, 33g protein, 0g fiber)

Simple and easy to make, this recipe is a must to try on this menu. Brazilian Picanha is a delight for the dinner table.

Ingredients (6 servings)
3 ⅓ lbs. of Picanha roast
2 tablespoons of olive oil
3 tablespoons of coarse salt

Preparation
At 390 degrees F, preheat your oven. Place the roast in a roasting pan. Rub it with salt and olive liberally. Add a splash of water to this pan and bake the roast for 70 minutes in the oven. Slice and serve warm.

Brazilian Corn Chowder (Sopa De Milho Verde)

Preparation time: 5 minutes
Cook time: 20 minutes
Nutrition facts (per serving): 365 Cal (32g fat, 29g protein, 2g fiber)

This corn and potato chowder is one of the traditional Brazilian entrées that is made mainly out of yogurt, corn, chicken broth and sausage.

Ingredients (6 servings)
2 tablespoon tablespoons of vegetable oil
½ white onion, chopped
3 garlic cloves, minced
6 cups of chicken broth
1 potato, peeled and diced
1 (29 oz.) can of sweet whole kernel corn drained
1 ½ teaspoon of salt
1 ½ teaspoon of black pepper
½ cup of plain yogurt
2 hot Italian sausage links, cooked and diced
4 tablespoons of fresh chives, chopped

Preparation
Sauté the onion with oil in a suitable pot for 4 minutes. Stir in the garlic and cook for 1 minute. Add the broth and cook to a simmer. Add the potato, 2 ¼ cups corn kernels, black pepper, and salt and cook for 12 minutes. Blend this soup with the yogurt in a blender. Add 1 cup of corn kernels and return the soup to the pan. Cook until warm and then garnish with the sausage and the chives. Serve warm.

Brazilian Minestrone

Preparation time: 5 minutes
Cook time: 22 minutes
Nutrition facts (per serving): 116 Cal (3g fat, 11g protein, 0.8g fiber)

A perfect mix of pasta, tomatoes and black beans in one meal is all that you need to expand your Brazilian menu. Simple and easy to make, this recipe is a must to try.

Ingredients (6 servings)
5 strips of smoked bacon, chopped
½ onion, chopped
⅓ cup of carrots, diced
⅓ cup of celery, diced
1 can of black beans
4 cups of beef stock
1 cup of canned tomatoes and their juice
Salt and black pepper, to taste
1 cup of rigatoni pasta
1 bay leaf
Chopped cilantro, to taste

Preparation
Sauté the bacon in a large pan for 5 minutes. Stir in the onions and cook for 5 minutes. Add the celery and carrots and then cook for 5 minutes. Stir in the tomatoes, beef stock, black pepper, salt, beans, bay leaf, and pasta and then cook to a boil. Cover and reduce its heat to medium-low then cook for 12 minutes. Discard the bay leave and garnish with cilantro and serve warm.

Macarronada Com Requeijão (Brazilian Mac And Cheese)

Preparation time: 10 minutes
Cook time: 35 minutes
Nutrition facts (per serving): 232 Cal (10g fat, 28g protein, 6g fiber)

This Brazilian mac and cheese will melt your heart away with its epic flavors. This meal is filled with creamy flavors.

Ingredients (6 servings)
16 oz. penne pasta, cooked and drained
1 tablespoon of olive oil
2 garlic cloves, minced
¼ cup of red wine
1-½ cup of tomato sauce
Salt and pepper, to taste
¼ cup basil, shredded
½ cup of heavy cream
8.5 oz. cheese spread
8 oz. mozzarella cheese, shredded
8 oz. rotisserie chicken
⅓ cup of Parmesan cheese, shredded

Preparation
At 350 degrees F, preheat your oven. Cook the pasta as per the package's instruction and then drain. Sauté the garlic with the oil in a deep pan for almost 1 minute. Add the wine and cook for 1 minute. Add the basil, black pepper, salt, and tomato sauce and then cook to a boil. Cover, reduce the heat, and cook for5 minutes. Add the mozzarella cheese, cheese spread, and cream and then cook until melted. Mix well and add the chicken. Spread the chicken mixture

and the pasta in a baking dish and drizzle Parmesan on top. Cover with a foil and bake for 20 minutes in the oven. Uncover and continue bake for 5 minutes. Serve warm.

Pizza A Portuguesa

Preparation time: 15 minutes
Cook time: 10 minutes
Nutrition facts (per serving): 139 Cal (0g fat, 8g protein, 2g fiber)

Do you want to enjoy a pizza with a Brazilian twist? Then try this olive and egg topped pizza recipe. You can serve it with a fresh kale or a cucumber salad on the side.

Ingredients (6 servings)
1 (12- inch) store-bought pizza crust
Olive oil, to brush
⅓ cup tomato sauce
3 cups of mozzarella cheese shredded
10 thin slices of deli smoked ham
6-8 slices of chorizo sausage stir-fried
1 large tomato, sliced
1 medium yellow onion, sliced
½ green bell pepper small, diced
2 large hard-boiled eggs
6-8 pitted black olives
Fresh oregano, to taste
1 pinch of salt
1 pinch of black pepper

Preparation
At 425 degrees F, preheat your oven. Layer a round baking sheet with parchment paper. Spread one pizza crust on a baking sheet and top it with the oil, tomato sauce, cheese, ham, sausage, onion, and tomatoes. Add the egg pieces, black olives, oregano, black pepper, and salt. Bake the pizza for 10 minutes. Serve warm.

Brazilian Beans

Preparation time: 10 minutes
Cook time: 55 minutes
Nutrition facts (per serving): 236 Cal (12g g fat, 5g protein, 3g fiber)

The famous Brazilian beans are another special entrée to try on the menu. Cook them at home with these healthy ingredients and enjoy.

Ingredients (8 servings)
2 cups of dried carioca beans
8 cups of water
2 bay leaves
3 strips of bacon, chopped
1 medium onion, chopped
4 garlic cloves, minced
Salt, to taste

Preparation
Add the beans, water, and bay leaves to an Instant Pot. Cover and seal the lid and then pressure cook the beans for 30 minutes. Once done, release the pressure completely and then remove the lid. Sauté the bacon in a large-deep skillet until brown. Stir in the onion and the garlic and sauté for 5 minutes. Add the cooked beans and their broth and then cook for 20 minutes on medium-low heat. Discard the bay leaf and then adjust the seasoning with salt. Serve warm.

Skirt Steak

Preparation time: 10 minutes
Cook time: 6 minutes
Nutrition facts (per serving): 236 Cal (5g fat, 23g protein, 1g fiber)

You can prepare this skirt steak with warm tortillas and the famous Brazilian chopped salad. Keep the chimichurri sauce prepared and pour over the steak before serving.

Ingredients (2 servings)
Coarse salt, to taste
1 ½ lbs. skirt steak trimmed, cut into half
Black pepper, to taste
½ lime, juiced

Preparation
Rub the steak with black pepper, lime juice, and salt. Set a pan over medium heat. Grease it with cooking spray and cook the steak for 3 minutes per side. Serve warm.

Cold Chicken Sandwich (Sanduíche Natural De Frango)

Preparation time: 10 minutes
Nutrition facts (per serving): 481 Cal (16g fat, 29g protein, 2g fiber)

The traditional cold chicken sandwich is here to add flavors to your dinner table, but this time with a mix of chicken and raisins filled sandwich. You can try it as an effortless entrée with all sorts of breads.

Ingredients (2 servings)
¾ cup of rotisserie chicken, shredded
⅓ cup of light mayonnaise
2 tablespoons of ketchup
1 teaspoon of fresh lemon juice
½ cup of carrots, peeled and shredded
¼ cup of raisins
1 pinch of salt
1 pinch of black pepper
4 slices of whole wheat bread

Preparation
Mix of shredded chicken with black pepper, salt, raisins, carrots, lemon juice, ketchup, and mayo in a bowl. Top half of the whole-wheat bread slices with the cheese mixture and place the other bread slices on top. Slice and serve.

Brazilian Pork Ribs (Costela De Porco Assada)

Preparation time: 15 minutes
Cook time: 2 hours 15 minutes
Nutrition facts (per serving): 365 Cal (17g fat, 25g protein, 5.4g fiber)

It's about time to try some classic pork ribs on the menu and make it more diverse and flavorsome. Serve warm with your favorite herbs on top.

Ingredients (8 servings)
4 teaspoons of salt
4 garlic cloves, minced
1 medium white onion, chopped
1 teaspoon of black pepper
1-½ teaspoon of Dijon mustard
1-½ teaspoon of Worcestershire sauce
1 teaspoon of dried oregano
¼ teaspoon of ground cumin
1 teaspoon of malagueta pepper
½ cup of apple cider vinegar
4 pounds of pork spareribs
Vegetable oil, for brushing

Preparation
Blend the salt, garlic, onion, black pepper, and the rest of the ingredients, except for the spare ribs. At 350 degrees F, preheat your oven. Place the ribs on a baking sheet and drizzle the marinade on top. Rub well, cover and marinate for 1 hour. Cover the pan with a foil sheet and bake for 1 hour 50 minutes. Increase the

oven temperature to 425 degrees F. to preheat your oven. Uncover and roast for 25 minutes. Serve warm.

Pan Fried Collard Greens (Couve A Mineira)

Preparation time: 15 minutes
Cook time: 14 minutes
Nutrition facts (per serving): 229 Cal (7g fat, 24g protein, 0.6g fiber)

Brazilian pan fried collard greens meal is great to complete your menu. Specifically, this one is beneficial on a nutritious diet.

Ingredients (4 servings)
2 bunches of collard greens
6 strips of smoked bacon, diced
4 garlic cloves, minced
Salt and black pepper, to taste
1 teaspoon of chicken bouillon powder

Preparation
Blanch the collard greens in 6 cups boiling water for 3 minutes and then drain. Sauté the bacon in a suitable skillet for 7 minutes. Stir in the garlic and sauté for almost 30 seconds. Add the collard greens, black pepper, salt, and bouillon powder. Cook for 3 minutes. Serve warm.

Ham And Cheese Baked Rice

Preparation time: 15 minutes
Cook time: 30 minutes
Nutrition facts (per serving): 338 Cal (10g fat, 33g protein, 3g fiber)

Now you can quickly make flavorsome Brazilian baked rice at home and serve it as a fancy meal for you and your guest.

Ingredients (4 servings)
2 large egg yolks
2½ cups of heavy whipping cream
½ small onion, diced
1 cup carrots, shredded
1 cup fresh parsley, chopped
1 teaspoon of salt
1 pinch of black pepper
8 oz. of mozzarella cheese, shredded
8 oz. of chopped deli ham
2 cups of cooked white rice
1 cup of Parmesan cheese, shredded

Preparation
At 350 degrees F, preheat your oven. Grease a suitable baking dish with butter and then dust with flour. Blend the yolks with the cream in a bowl. Stir in the rice, ham, mozzarella, black pepper, salt, 1 cup of parsley, carrot, and an onion. Mix well and then spread this mixture into the baking dish. Drizzle Parmesan on top and bake for 30 minutes. Garnish with parsley. Serve warm.

Brazilian Chicken Pot Pie

Preparation time: 10 minutes
Cook time: 52 minutes
Nutrition facts (per serving): 378 Cal (11g fat, 25g protein, 3g fiber)

If you haven't tried this chicken pot pie before, then here comes a simple and easy to cook recipe that you can easily recreate in your kitchen with minimum efforts.

Ingredients (4 servings)
Chicken Filling
2 tablespoons of olive oil
2 medium onions, chopped
2 garlic cloves, minced
2 tomatoes, chopped
2 pounds of chicken breast, cooked and shredded
½ cup of chopped green olives
1 cup of corn
1 cup of green peas
1 cup of hearts of palm, chopped
1 cup of tomato sauce
A couple of dashes of hot sauce
2 cups of chicken broth
1 tablespoon of flour mixed with ⅓ cup milk
½ cup of chopped parsley
Salt and black pepper, to taste

Crust
5 cups of flour
1 teaspoon of salt
3 egg yolks
½ cup of cold water

3 sticks of butter (12 oz.) cut into smaller pieces
1 egg yolk, beaten, for brushing

Preparation
Sauté the onions and the garlic with oil in a deep skillet for 2 minutes. Add the tomatoes and cook for 5 minutes. Stir in the corn, peas, and the rest of the filling ingredients then cook for 10 minutes. Mix well and keep it aside. Mix the flour and the rest of the crust ingredients in a bowl. Knead the prepared dough, cover and leave for 20 minutes. At 350 degrees F, preheat your oven. Take ⅔ of this dough and spread it into a 12 inch round. Place it in a 9 inch pan and press it against the walls. Poke some holes in the crust and add the prepared filling in it. Roll the remaining dough into a 9 inch round and place it over the filling. Cut a cross on top and brush it with the egg yolk. Bake for 35 minutes in the oven. Slice and serve warm.

Brazilian Saffron Rice With Chicken (Galinhada)

Preparation time: 10 minutes
Cook time: 37 minutes
Nutrition facts (per serving): 212 Cal (8g fat, 5g protein, 2g fiber)

Try making this delicious saffron rice with some delicious chicken to enjoy the best of the Brazilian flavors at home.

Ingredients (4 servings)
2 lbs. of boneless chicken thighs
2 teaspoons of salt
½ teaspoon of black pepper
½ teaspoon of ground cumin
½ cup of hot water
5 saffron threads
2 tablespoons of olive oil
1 small white onion, diced
1 large green bell pepper, diced
4 garlic cloves, minced
2 cups of white rice long-grain, parboiled
½ cup of white wine
3 cups of chicken broth
1 teaspoon of tomato paste
1 bay leaf
3 large tomatoes, diced
¾ cup of fresh peas
½ lemon
2 tablespoons of green onions, chopped

Preparation

Rub the chicken with cumin, black pepper, and salt. Soak all the saffron threads in hot water in a bowl for 30 minutes. Sear the chicken thighs in a pan greased with 2 tablespoons of oil for 4 minutes per side. Then keep it aside. Sauté the bell pepper and the onion in the same pan for 4 minutes. Stir in the garlic and sauté for 1 minute. Add the rice and cook for 2 minutes. Add the wine and cook for 2 minutes. Add the tomato paste, bay leaf, broth, and saffron. Cook to a boil, cover, and cook on a simmer for 15 minutes. Add the peas, tomatoes, lemon juice, and chicken on top. Cover and leave for 5 minutes. Garnish with herbs and serve warm.

Creamy Corn Gratin (Creme De Milho Gratinado)

Preparation time: 10 minutes
Cook time: 35 minutes
Nutrition facts (per serving): 396 Cal (13g fat, 22g protein, 4g fiber)

This loaded corn gratin brings all the delicious Brazilian delights in one place, including cheese, corn, and milk.

Ingredients (6 servings)
½ tablespoon of unsalted butter
½ cup of whole milk
½ cup of sour cream
2 cups of corn kernels
3 large eggs
2 tablespoons of all-purpose flour
½ teaspoon of salt
½ teaspoon of pepper
¼ teaspoon of baking soda
1 cup of provolone cheese, shredded
½ cup of Parmesan cheese, shredded

Preparation
At 375 degrees F, preheat your oven. Grease a 1 ½ quart gratin dish with butter. Blend the corn kernels with crème and milk in a blender until smooth. Stir in the baking soda, black pepper, salt, flour, and egg and then mix well. Stir in the provolone cheese and mix well. Spread this mixture in the gratin dish and top it with the Parmesan cheese. Bake for 35 minutes in the oven. Serve warm.

Brazilian Potato Cod Casserole

Preparation time: 10 minutes
Cook time: 40 minutes
Nutrition facts (per serving): 701 Cal (31g fat, 77g protein, 6g fiber)

Make this Brazilian cod casserole in no time and enjoy it with some garnish on top. It has layers of cod, potatoes, and eggs, which make it super-rich.

Ingredients (6 servings)
2 pounds of dried salted codfish
4 Yukon Gold potatoes
3 tablespoons of butter
2 yellow onions, sliced
2 garlic cloves, chopped
½ cup of fresh parsley, chopped
¾ cup of olive oil
1 ½ teaspoon of red pepper flakes
Black pepper, to taste
4 hard-cooked eggs, chopped
10 pitted green olives
10 pitted black olives

Preparation
Soak the cod in salted water for 24 hours and then remove it from the water. Transfer the cod to a pan and pour in enough water to cover. Cook the cod for 5 minutes and then transfer to a plate. Add the potatoes and cook for 20 minutes until soft. Meanwhile, remove the cod skin and bones. Flake the cod in a bowl using a bowl. Mix the black pepper, red pepper flakes, 1 tablespoon of parsley, 1 garlic clove, and olive oil in a small bowl. Drain the potatoes and slice them. Sauté the onions with butter in a skillet until caramelized. Stir

in the garlic and sauté for almost 1 minute. Place half the onion slices in a greased 8x11 casserole dish and then top them with half of the cod and half of the onion's mixture. Then repeat the layers with the other half of potato slices, cod, and onion. Bake the casserole for 15 minutes. Garnish with hard-cooked eggs, black and green olives, and parsley. Serve.

Brazilian Pork Stew

Preparation time: 15 minutes
Cook time: 15 minutes
Nutrition facts (per serving): 315 Cal (12g fat, 28 protein, 2g fiber)

This pork stew is quite famous in the region. In fact, it's a must to try because of its nutritional content.

Ingredients (6 servings)
1 ½ cups of dry white wine
1 teaspoon of paprika
2 ½ teaspoon of salt
¼ teaspoon of black pepper
2 garlic cloves, peeled and halved
1 bay leaf
2 pounds of pork loin, cut into cubes
3 teaspoons of olive oil
2 onions, peeled and sliced
2 teaspoons of garlic, chopped
2 tomatoes, peeled and chopped
¼ teaspoon of crushed red pepper flakes
24 small clams in the shell, scrubbed
¼ cup of fresh parsley, chopped

Preparation
Add the black pepper, salt, paprika, and wine to a bowl and then mix well. Stir in the meat, bay leaf, and garlic cloves and then mix well. Cover and marinate the meat for 6 hours. Transfer the prepared pork to a plate and discard the bay leaf and garlic. Sauté the pork cubes with 1 teaspoon of oil in a large skillet and sauté until brown. Transfer to a bowl. Pour the remaining marinade into the skillet, cook to a boil, and then cook on a simmer until it is reduced to half. Pour the marinade over the pork. Sauté the onion with 2 teaspoons

of oil in a 6-quart pan for 5 minutes. Stir in the red pepper, tomatoes, and garlic, then sauté for 5 minutes. Add the tomato sauce and clams and then cover the pan. Cook until the clams open. Stir in the juices and the pork, and then cook for 5 minutes on a simmer. Garnish with parsley. Enjoy.

Brazilian Clams

Preparation time: 10 minutes
Cook time: 15 minutes
Nutrition facts (per serving): 697 Cal (53g fat, 30g protein, 3g fiber)

The steamed clams are everything I was looking for. Sample this simple and easy to cook recipe today!

Ingredients (10 servings)
5 pounds clams in the shell, scrubbed
1 ½ pounds of chorizo, sliced
1 large onion, cut into wedges
1 (14.5 oz.) can of tomatoes, diced
2 cups of white wine
¼ cup of olive oil

Preparation
Add the clams to a stockpot and insert the wine, tomatoes, onion, and sausage. Cover and cook until the clams open up. Finally, drizzle olive oil on top. Serve.

Shrimp Stew

Preparation time: 15 minutes
Cook time: 10 minutes
Nutrition facts (per serving): 227 Cal (13g fat, 20g protein, 2g fiber)

You know until you try it! That's what people told me about this stew, and it indeed tasted more unique and flavorsome than shrimp stews I've sampled.

Ingredients (4 servings)
4 t tablespoons of butter
¼ cup of onion, chopped
½ cup of water
1 lemon, juiced
8 garlic cloves, chopped
2 (1.41 oz.) packages of sazon seasoning
Salt and black pepper, to taste
½ (12 oz.) of bottle beer
2 teaspoons of hot sauce
1-pound medium shrimp, peeled and deveined

Preparation
Sauté the onion with butter in a suitable saucepan over medium heat for 5 minutes. Stir in the black pepper, salt, sazon, garlic, lemon juice, and water and then cook for 2 minutes. Stir in the beer and hot sauce and then cook the mixture to a boil. Stir in the shrimp and cook for almost 3 minutes. Serve warm.

Brazilian Beef Stew

Preparation time: 15 minutes
Cook time: 80 minutes
Nutrition facts (per serving): 398 Cal (12g fat, 27g protein, 4g fiber)

This beef stew is loved by all, young and adult. It's quite simple and quick to make. This delight is great to serve at dinner tables.

Ingredients (4 servings)
2 tablespoons of olive oil
1-pound of stew meat, cut into cubes
1 of tablespoon all-purpose flour
8 garlic cloves, minced
2 bay leaves
1 pinch of black pepper
1 pinch of salt
1 onion, chopped
1 green bell pepper, chopped
1 carrot, chopped
1 pinch paprika
½ fresh tomato, chopped
1 cup of white wine
1 cup of water
2 sprigs of fresh parsley
3 red potatoes, peeled and cubed
1 sweet potato, peeled and cubed
1 (14.5 oz.) can of green beans, drained

Preparation
Dust the beef with the flour. Add oil, dusted beef, black pepper, bay leaves, and garlic to a suitable saucepan. Sauté until the beef is brown. Stir in the paprika, carrot, green pepper, and onion, then

sauté for 5 minutes. Add the parsley, water, wine, and tomatoes, cover, and cook for 30 minutes on a simmer. Add the red potatoes, green beans, and sweet potatoes. Lastly, cook for 45 minutes. Serve warm.

Seafood Bread Stew

Preparation time: 5 minutes
Cook time: 15 minutes
Nutrition facts (per serving): 433 Cal (6.8g fat, 73g protein, 3g fiber)

Try this seafood bread stew for dinner as the bread is infused with amazing flavors of seafood broth. Serve warm with your favorite sauces.

Ingredients (6 servings)
21 oz. (600g) of clams
21 oz. (600g) of cockle
22 oz. of peeled shrimps
21 oz. (600g) of hard Eve bread
4 garlic cloves
1 tablespoon of oil
1 bunch of coriander, chopped
4 eggs
Salt, to taste
Black pepper, to taste
Chili, to taste

Preparation
Boil the shrimp in salted water for almost 2 minutes, then transfer to a bowl. Add the clams and cockles to the boiling water and cook to a boil. Spread the bread pieces in a bowl and pour the clams water over it to soak. Sauté the garlic with olive oil in a suitable saucepan until brown. Stir in the coriander and squeeze the bread. Add the shrimps, eggs, clams, cockle, chili, black pepper, salt, and serve.

Brazilian Shrimp Fry

Preparation time: 5 minutes
Cook time: 25 minutes
Nutrition facts (per serving): 147 Cal (3g fat, 20g protein, 3g fiber)

Simple and easy to make, this recipe is a must to try on this menu. Brazilian shrimp fry is a delight for the dinner table.

Ingredients (6 servings)
1 tablespoon of olive oil
1 onion, chopped
3 garlic cloves, minced
1 (12 oz.) can of ale
5 sprigs parsley, stemmed and chopped
2 teaspoons of tomato paste
2 teaspoons of Brazilian hot pepper sauce
1 cube of chicken bouillon
1 teaspoon of ground paprika
2 pounds of large shrimp, deveined
1 teaspoon of salt

Preparation
Sauté the onion and garlic with olive oil in a skillet for 5 minutes. Stir in the paprika, half of the ale, chicken bouillon, hot pepper sauce, tomato paste, and parsley, and then cook for 5 minutes. Stir in the shrimp, salt, and the remaining ale. Cook for 15-20 minutes until the shrimp change their color. Serve warm.

Chicken Sausage Rice

Preparation time: 5 minutes
Cook time: 50 minutes
Nutrition facts (per serving): 539 Cal (20g fat, 26g protein, 4g fiber)

This rice meal is one of the traditional Brazilian entrées made with rice, sausage, and ham, etc.

Ingredients (6 servings)
2 tablespoons of vegetable oil
1 onion, chopped
½ pound of chicken thighs, diced
½ pound of chicken drumsticks, boneless and diced
2 teaspoons of salt
7 oz. ham, cubed and cooked
2 pork sausages, smoked, sliced
2 links of pork sausage, sliced
3 cups of rice, rinsed and drained
4 tomatoes, chopped
1 red bell pepper, sliced
2 spring onions, chopped
1 teaspoon of parsley, chopped
6 cups of water
2 cubes of chicken bouillon
3 leaves of cabbage, sliced
1 tablespoon of olive oil

Preparation
Sauté the onion with drumsticks and chicken thighs in a cooking pot for 10 minutes. Stir in the sausages and ham, and then cook for 10 minutes. Add the parsley, salt, spring onion, red bell pepper, tomatoes, water, chicken bouillon, and rice. Partially cover the pot

and cook on a simmer for 15 minutes. Add the sliced cabbage and cook for another 15 minutes. Garnish with olive oil and serve warm.

Brazilian Beef Skewers

Preparation time: 15 minutes
Cook time: 8 minutes
Nutrition facts (per serving): 190 Cal (7.8g fat, 23.8g protein, 3g fiber)

The classic Brazilian beef skewers are here to complete your Brazilian menu. This meal can be served on all special occasions and festive celebrations, especially on BBQ night.

Ingredients (6 servings)
¾ cup of red wine
8 garlic cloves
6 bay leaves, crumbled
2 tablespoons of salt
Black pepper, to taste
3 of pounds beef sirloin steak, cubed

Preparation
Mix the black pepper, salt, bay leaves, and red wine in a large suitable bowl. Toss in the sirloin cubes and cover to refrigerate for 8 hours. Preheat and prepare a grill over medium-high heat. Thread the beef on the skewers and grill the beef for 4 minutes per side. Serve warm.

Brazilian Rice And Beans

Preparation time: 15 minutes
Cook time: 40 minutes
Nutrition facts (per serving): 562 Cal (34g fat, 19g protein, 3.2g fiber)

The Brazilian rice and bean recipe are here to complete your Brazilian menu. This meal can be served and enjoyed on all sorts of celebrations.

Ingredients (4 servings)
½ cup of butter
1 large onion, chopped
1 green bell pepper, chopped
1 red bell pepper, chopped
1-pound linguica sausage, cut into cubes
1 teaspoon of black pepper
1 teaspoon of dried basil
½ teaspoon of dried oregano
1 (15.5 oz.) can of shelled beans
2 ½ cups of water
2 cups of white rice

Preparation
Sauté the onion, bell peppers, oregano, basil, black pepper, and sauté in a cooking pot for 15 minutes. Add the beans and cook for 5 minutes. Stir in rice and water, cover, and cook for 25 minutes on low heat until the rice is soft. Serve warm.

Brazilian Beef Roast

Preparation time: 15 minutes
Cook time: 4 hours 30 minutes
Nutrition facts (per serving): 464 Cal (32g fat, 34g protein, 5g fiber)

It's about time to try some classic beef roast on the menu and make it more diverse and flavorsome. Serve warm with your favorite herbs on top.

Ingredients (6 servings)
1 (3 pounds) of beef pot roast
1 onion, diced
1 cup of fresh mint leaves
2 garlic cloves, minced
2 teaspoons of ground cinnamon
2 teaspoons of ground allspice
2 bay leaves
Salt and black pepper, to taste
Water, to cover
1 head cabbage, quartered

Preparation
Add the pot roast, bay leaves, allspice, cinnamon, garlic, mint, onion, black pepper, and salt to a cooking pot and pour enough water over the pot roast to cover it. Cook the meat for 4 hours on a simmer. Add the cabbage wedges and cook for 30 minutes on a simmer. Serve warm.

Brazilian Beef Steaks

Preparation time: 15 minutes
Cook time: 6 minutes
Nutrition facts (per serving): 467 Cal (39g fat, 21g protein, 3g fiber)

This beef steaks recipe is always an easy way to add extra proteins and nutrients to your menu. Asa result, prepare this in just a few minutes.

Ingredients (6 servings)
¾ cup of red wine
¼ cup of water
10 garlic cloves, chopped
1 tablespoon of chile paste
½ teaspoon of white pepper
½ teaspoon of salt
6 (4 oz.) beef tenderloin steaks
⅓ cup vegetable oil

Preparation
Mix the beef with salt, white pepper, chile paste, water, and red wine in a medium bowl. Add the beef to a greased skillet for 2 minutes per side. Once seared, add the marinade to the beef and cook for 2 minutes on a boil. Serve warm.

Brazilian Glazed Chicken

Preparation time: 15 minutes
Cook time: 45 minutes
Nutrition facts (per serving): 492 Cal (35g fat, 40g protein, 6g fiber)

If you haven't tried the Brazilian chicken, then here comes an authentic, simple, and easy to cook recipe that you can recreate easily at home in minimum time.

Ingredients (4 servings)
¼ cup of lemon juice
4 tablespoons of olive oil
4 garlic cloves, peeled
1 tablespoon of paprika
1 teaspoon of dried oregano
1 teaspoon of sea salt
1 teaspoon of chili powder
1 teaspoon of red pepper flakes
1 bay leaf
½ teaspoon of black pepper
4 chicken leg quarters
1 pinch of sea salt

Preparation
Blend the black pepper, bay leaf, red pepper flakes, chili powder, 1 teaspoon salt, oregano, paprika, garlic, lemon juice, and oil in a blender for 1 minute. Score the chicken legs with a knife and place them in a bowl. Pour the marinade over the chicken. Rub the chicken with the paste and refrigerate for 8 hours. Spread the chicken in a baking dish and cover with aluminum foil. Bake the chicken for almost 25 minutes at 350 degrees F. Turn the chicken,

baste with the marinade, cover again, and bake again for 20 minutes. Serve warm.

Wine Garlic Pork

Preparation time: 15 minutes
Cook time: 35 minutes
Nutrition facts (per serving): 291 Cal (20g fat, 18g protein, 2g fiber)

This garlic pork is famous for its unique taste and aroma, and now you can bring those exotic flavors home by using this recipe.

Ingredients (6 servings)
1 ½ cups of red wine vinegar
¾ cup of red wine
7 garlic cloves, crushed
½ teaspoon of dried thyme
3 bay leaves
8 whole cloves
2 tablespoons of black pepper, ground
2 teaspoons of salt
1 (3 pounds) boneless pork shoulder, cubed
2 tablespoons of vegetable oil

Preparation
Mix the thyme, salt, black pepper, cloves, bay leaves, garlic, red wine, and red wine vinegar in a bowl. Add this prepared mixture to a Ziplock bag along with pork, seal the bag, and shake the bag to cover the pork. Marinate the seasoned pork for 2 days in the refrigerator and shake the bag after every 12 hours. At 350 degrees F, preheat your oven. Transfer the pork and ½ cup marinade to a baking dish. Bake the pork for 20 minutes in the oven, then remove the meat from the marinade. Sauté the pork with oil in a skillet over medium heat and for 15 minutes until brown. Serve warm.

Braised Chicken

Preparation time: 15 minutes
Cook time: 65 minutes
Nutrition facts (per serving): 540 Cal (39g fat, 37g protein, 8g fiber)

The delicious braised chicken always tastes great when you cook the chicken with lots of herbs and spices using this recipe.

Ingredients (5 servings)
1 tablespoon of olive oil
¼-pound linguica sausage, sliced
½ onion, sliced
½ green bell pepper, chopped
2 pounds of chicken parts
¾ teaspoon of fresh oregano, chopped
⅛ teaspoon of fresh basil, chopped
½ teaspoon of salt
¼ teaspoon of black pepper
½ cup of dry white wine
½ cup and 1 teaspoon of chicken broth
1 bay leaf
⅛ teaspoon of red pepper flakes
½ orange, cut into wedges

Preparation
Sauté the bell pepper, onion, and sausage with oil in a Dutch oven for 10 minutes transfer to a plate. Rub the chicken with black pepper, salt, basil, and oregano and sear the chicken for 10 minutes in the same pot over medium-high heat. Add the vegetable mixture, sausage, red pepper flakes, bay leaves, broth, and wine, and then cook the mixture to a boil. Reduce the heat, cover, and cook for 45 minutes on a simmer. Serve warm.

Desserts

Corn Bundt Cake (Bolo De Milho De Liquidificador)

Preparation time: 10 minutes
Cook time: 35 minutes
Nutrition facts (per serving): 41 Cal (3g fat, 1g protein, 1.4g fiber)

Corn Bundt Cake is here to make your meal special. Savor the delicious and healthy combination of ingredients.

Ingredients (6 servings)
1 cup of yellow corn
1 cup of coconut milk
¼ cup of water
3 large eggs
1 stick and 1 tablespoon unsalted butter, melted
1 ⅓ cup granulated sugar
2 cups of coarse yellow corn meal
2 tablespoons of unsweetened coconut flakes
3 tablespoons of Parmesan cheese, grated
1 pinch of salt
1 tablespoon of baking powder

Preparation
At 350 degrees F, preheat your oven. Grease a 10 inch baking pan. Blend the corn and the rest of the ingredients in a blender until smooth. Spread the batter in the pan and bake for 35 minutes. Allow the cake to cool. Slice and serve.

Papaya Cream With Cassis (Creme De Papaya Com Cassis)

Preparation time: 15 minutes
Cook time: 10 minutes
Nutrition facts (per serving): 456 Cal (15g fat, 6g protein, 0.7g fiber)

If you haven't tried this papaya cream, then here comes a simple and easy to cook recipe that you can easily recreate in your kitchen with minimum efforts.

Ingredients (4 servings)
Papaya Cream
2 cups of ripe papaya peeled, deseeded and cubed
2 scoops of vanilla ice cream
2 tablespoons of cassis cream

Berry Coulis
⅓ cup of blackberries
⅓ cup of raspberries
⅓ cup of strawberries
4 tablespoons of powdered sugar
1 cup of water
Juice from ½ lemon

Preparation
Blend the papaya cream ingredients in a blender and refrigerate for 1 hour. Meanwhile, mix all the berries, water, lemon juice, and sugar in a pan and cook for 10 minutes with occasional stirring. Divide the papaya cream in the serving cups and top them with the berry mixture. Make swirls on top and serve.

Tapioca Breadsticks (Biscoito De Polvilho)

Preparation time: 15 minutes
Cook time: 15 minutes
Nutrition facts (per serving): 635 Cal (38g fat, 10g protein, 2g fiber)

This new version of Brazilian tapioca breadsticks is amazing, and it's super simple and easy to cook. It's brilliant for all the breadstick lovers.

Ingredients (8 servings)
4 cups of tapioca flour
⅓ cup of Parmesan cheese, grated
½ cup of whole milk
½ cup of vegetable oil
½ tablespoon and 1 teaspoon of salt
½ tablespoon of fresh rosemary, chopped
3 large eggs

Preparation
Mix the Parmesan n cheese and tapioca flour in a large bowl. Mix the rosemary, salt, oil and milk in a suitable saucepan and cook to a simmer. Stir in the flour mixture and mix until smooth. Beat the eggs and slowly pour into pan and mix for 4 minutes into a smooth dough. At 350 degrees F, preheat your oven. Grease your hands and make 2 tablespoon sized dough balls then roll each into a breadstick. Place the breadsticks on a baking sheet and bake for 15 minutes in the oven. Allow the breadsticks to cool. Serve.

Apple Crumb Cake

Preparation time: 15 minutes
Cook time: 40 minutes
Nutrition facts (per serving): 187 Cal (9g fat, 2g protein, 1g fiber)

This apple crumb cake is always an easy way to add extra flavors and nutrients to your menu. Make this one in just a few minutes.

Ingredients (8 servings)
Cake Batter
2 cups of all-purpose flour
¾ cup of white sugar
2 teaspoons of baking powder
1 dash of salt
1 tablespoon of shortening, melted
3 tablespoons of unsalted butter, melted
1 large egg
1 cup of heavy cream
1 tablespoon of vanilla extract
3 medium baking tart apples, cored, and cut into ⅛ slices

Streusel Topping
¼ cup all-purpose flour
2 tablespoon of sugar
½ teaspoon of ground cinnamon
1-½ tablespoon of cold unsalted butter, cut into pieces
½ tablespoon of heavy whipping cream
1 teaspoon of pure vanilla extract

Garnish
⅓ cup of caramel sauce

Preparation

At 350 degrees F, preheat your oven. Grease a suitable 8x8 inch baking pan with cooking spray. Mix the streusel topping ingredients in a bowl. Mix all the cake batter ingredients in a bowl until smooth. Spread the cake batter in the baking pan and top it with the apple slices and the streusel topping. Bake this cake for 40 minutes in the oven. Allow the cake to cool and slice to serve.

Bread Pudding (Pudim De Pão)

Preparation time: 15 minutes
Cook time: 40 minutes
Nutrition facts (per serving): 142 Cal (4g fat, 4g protein, 3g fiber)

Here's a delicious and savory combination of bread and milk cream that you must add to your menu.

Ingredients (6 servings)
5 cups of stale French bread, diced
3 cups of warm milk
4 eggs
2 cups of sugar
1 teaspoon of vanilla extract
⅓ cup of light corn syrup warm

Preparations
At 350 degrees F, preheat your oven. Soak the bread in warm milk in a bowl for 5 minutes. Stir in the rest of the ingredients, except for the syrup. Heat the syrup in a suitable saucepan and pour in a 10 inch ring pan. Pour the bread mixture in this pan and bake for 40 minutes. Allow the cake to cool, flip over the plate, and slice to serve.

Brazilian Carrot Cake

Preparation time: 15 minutes
Cook time: 55 minutes
Nutrition facts (per serving): 336 Cal (18g fat, 0g protein, 1.7g fiber)

A perfect mix of carrot cake and chocolate topping on the outside is worth trying. Serve with your favorite toasted nuts.

Ingredients (6 servings)
Cake batter
17.5 oz. of carrots, peeled and chopped
1 cup of vegetable oil
1 of tablespoon pure vanilla extract
3 large eggs
1 large egg yolk
2 cups of sugar
2 ⅛ cups of all-purpose flour
2 teaspoons of baking powder
Pinch of salt

Chocolate sauce
½ cup of milk chocolate chips
1 cup of milk
2 teaspoons of cornstarch mixed with 2 teaspoons of water
1 tablespoon of unsalted butter
1 tablespoon of honey
1 tablespoon of vanilla extract

Preparation
At 350 degrees F, preheat your oven. Grease a round rings mold and dust it with flour. Blend the carrot, half of the sugar, eggs, yolk, oil, and vanilla in a blender. Transfer this eggs mixture to a bowl and

stir in rest of the ingredients. Mix well and spread this batter in the prepared mold and bake for 55 minutes in the oven. Mix the chocolate chips, and milk in a suitable saucepan then cook until melted. Stir in the cornstarch mixture, butter, honey and vanilla then cook until the sauce thickens. Allow the cake to cool and pour the chocolate sauce on top. Serve.

Brigadeiro Cookies

Preparation time: 15 minutes
Cook time: 8 minutes
Nutrition facts (per serving): 316 Cal (21g fat, 5g protein, 0g fiber)

Are you in a mood to have some loaded cookies on the menu? Well, you can serve these delicious brigadeiro cookies using this simple recipe.

Ingredients (14 servings)

1 (14-oz.) can of sweetened condensed milk
¼ cup of baking cocoa powder
2 tablespoons of unsalted butter
1 tablespoon of pure vanilla extract
14 Oreo sandwich cookies
Chocolate sprinkles, to coat

Preparation

Mix the milk with the cocoa powder in a pan and cook with stirring until smooth. Stir in the butter and vanilla and cook for 8 minutes until the mixture thickens. Allow this mixture to cool. Make 2 tablespoon sized cocoa dough balls and coat them with the sprinkles. Place a ball in between the two sides of a cookie sandwich. Serve.

No Bake Tapioca Cake

Preparation time: 10 minutes
Nutrition facts (per serving): 213 Cal (10g fat, 4g protein, 5g fiber)

This Tapioca cake is one delicious way to complete your Brazilian dessert menu, so here's a recipe for a delicious treat.

Ingredients (8 servings)
4 cups of whole milk
3 ¼ cups of tapioca
2 cups of sugar
2 ½ cups of sweetened coconut flakes
½ cup of canned coconut milk
1 ½ cans of sweetened condensed milk

Preparation
Boil the whole milk in a suitable saucepan. Stir in the coconut milk, coconut flakes, sugar, tapioca, and condensed milk. Mix and cook until the mixture thickens. Spread this mixture in a 10 cup ring pan, cover, and refrigerate for 2 hours. Run a knife around the cake and flip over onto the serving platter. Serve.

Brazilian Coconut Kisses (Beijinhos De Coco)

Preparation time: 10 minutes
Cook time: 8 minutes
Nutrition facts (per serving): 231 Cal (9.5g fat, 9.7g protein, 9g fiber)

Who doesn't like these kisses? Get ready to enjoy a heart-melting coconut dessert on this menu.

Ingredients (6 servings)
1 (14-oz.) can sweetened condensed milk
1 cup sweetened coconut flakes
½ tablespoon unsalted butter softened
1 teaspoon pure vanilla extract
Cloves for garnishing

Preparation
Mix the butter, coconut flakes, and condensed milk in a suitable saucepan. Cook for 8 minutes while stirring. Stir in the vanilla and allow the milk mixture to cool. Make small balls from this mixture with greased hands. Place each ball in a bonbon cup. Stick a clove on top of each ball and serve.

Avocado Mousse

Preparation time: 15 minutes
Nutrition facts (per serving): 119 Cal (9g fat, 4g protein, 0.5g fiber)

The famous avocado mousse recipe is here to make your Brazilian cuisine extra special. Serve it with some chopped nuts on top.

Ingredients (4 servings)
1 14-oz sweetened condensed milk
4 small avocados, peeled and pitted
2 limes juiced
2 tablespoon granulated sugar
1 tablespoon chopped pistachio

Preparation
Blend the milk, avocado, lime juice, and sugar in a blender until smooth. Divide this mouse into 4 ramekins and refrigerate for 2 hours. Garnish with pistachios and serve.

Brazilian Cornmeal Cake

Preparation time: 15 minutes
Cook time: 10 minutes
Nutrition facts (per serving): 411 Cal (9g fat, 11g protein, 7g fiber)

When you can't think of anything to serve as the dessert, then these delicious squares will help you to easily enjoy the authentic Brazilian flavors.

Ingredients (6 servings)
1 teaspoon butter
1 cup all-purpose flour
1 cup corn meal
1 tablespoon baking powder
¼ teaspoon salt
1 cup sugar
2 eggs
½ cup vegetable oil
1 cup whole milk

Preparation
At 350 degrees F, preheat your oven. Grease a Bundt cake with the butter. Mix the flour with the rest of the cake ingredients in a mixer. Spread this mixture in the pan and bake for 10 minutes. Allow it to cool, slice, and serve.

Moist Coconut Cake

Preparation time: 15 minutes
Cook time: 60 minutes
Nutrition facts (per serving): 286 Cal (11g fat, 2g protein, 3g fiber)

This moist coconut cake is a must-have as a dessert. So, with the help of this recipe, you can bake it in no time.

Ingredients (6 servings)
Cake
1 ½ sticks of butter, softened
2 cups sugar
4 eggs, yolks and eggs separated
1 teaspoon vanilla extract
2 ½ cups all-purpose flour
½ cup whole milk
1 (13.5 oz.) can coconut milk
1 tablespoon baking powder
1 pinch of salt

Sauce
1 (13 ½ oz.) can coconut milk
1 (14 oz.) can sweet condensed milk
2 cups coconut flakes

Preparation
At 350 degrees F, preheat your oven. Grease a suitable 9 inch cake pan with baking paper. Grease it with cooking spray and dust it with flour. Beat the egg whites in a suitable bowl until foamy and set them aside. Beat the egg yolks, sugar, and butter in the bowl of stand mixer. Beat for 5 minutes. Stir in the vanilla and mix well. Stir in the rest of the cake ingredients and mix until smooth. Fold in the egg whites, mix evenly, and then spread in the bake pan. Bake the cake

for 60 minutes. Allow the cake to cool. Mix the coconut milk, condensed milk, and coconut flakes in a pan and cook until thick. Pour the glaze over the cake. Slice and serve.

Chocolate Covered Cream Pie

Preparation time: 10 minutes
Cook time: 16 minutes
Nutrition facts (per serving): 227 Cal (15g fat, 11g protein, 2.1g fiber)

The chocolate covered cream pie is the best dessert in Brazilian cuisine. It's loaded with flavor as the pie is prepared with a graham crackers crust and cream filling inside.

Ingredients (8 servings)
Crust
30 squares honey graham crackers
1 ½ sticks of butter, softened
12 chocolate covered digestive cookies

Cream filling
3 egg yolks
1 (14 oz.) can sweet condensed milk
1 cup whole milk
1 (¼ oz.) package unflavored gelatin
½ cup cold water
1 ½ cups heavy cream

Chocolate ganache
1 (12 oz.) bag sweet chocolate chips
1 cup heavy cream

Preparation
Blend the graham crackers with the butter in a food processor and spread it in a 9 inch springform pan greased with a cooking spray. Cover and refrigerate this crust for 1 hour. Beat egg yolks with milk and sweet condensed milk in a suitable saucepan and cook to a boil. Reduce its heat and cook for 10 minutes until thicken. Mix the

gelatin and the cold water in a bowl and heat in the microwave for 5 seconds. Add this gelatin mixture to the cream mixture and cook until the mixture thickens. Beat the heavy cream in a bowl until fluffy. Add this cream to the milk mixture, mix evenly, and spread the mixture in the crust. Cover and refrigerate for 3 hours. For the ganache, add the cream and chocolate chips to a suitable saucepan and cook until the chocolate is melted. Pour this ganache over the pie, cover it again, and refrigerate for 1 hour. Serve.

Brazilian Flan

Preparation time: 15 minutes
Cook time: 1 hour 42 minutes
Nutrition facts (per serving): 228 Cal (6g fat, 4g protein, 3g fiber)

Brazilian flan is one good option to go for in the desserts. You can also keep it ready and stored as an instant dessert.

Ingredients (6 servings)
1 cup sugar
⅓ cup water
2 (14 oz.) cans sweet condensed milk
28 oz. whole milk
4 eggs
1 tablespoon vanilla extract

Preparation
At 375 degrees F, preheat your oven. Melt the butter in a pan and cook for 10 minutes until brown. Stir in the water and mix well. Spread this caramel in a 10 inch pan and allow it to cool. Mix the vanilla, eggs, milk, and condensed milk in a pan and cook for 2 minutes while stirring. Pour this mixture in to the pan, cover with a foil sheet, and bake for 1 ½ hour in the oven. Allow the flan to cool and flip over the serving plate. Serve.

Brazilian Fudge Balls (Traditional Brigadeiros)

Preparation time: 10 minutes
Nutrition facts (per serving): 233 Cal (15g fat, 15g protein, 3.1g fiber)

If you just can't figure out what to cook and make in a short time, then this treat is the perfect choice because it has a great taste and texture.

Ingredients (6 servings)
1 (14oz) can sweet condensed milk
4 tablespoon cocoa powder, sifted
2 tablespoon butter
A pinch of salt
Chocolate sprinkles, to coat

Preparation
Mix the butter, salt, cocoa powder, and condensed milk in a suitable saucepan. Cook over medium-low heat until it thickens. Allow this mixture to cool. Spread the sprinkles on a plate. Make small balls from the cocoa mixture with greased hands and coat them with the sprinkles. Serve.

Brazilian Cream Doughnuts

Preparation time: 15 minutes
Cook time: 10 minutes
Nutrition facts (per serving): 206 Cal (29g fat, 4g protein, 0.1g fiber)

The appetizing cream doughnuts make a great addition to the menu, and they look appeal when served at the table.

Ingredients (6 servings)
Dough
1 (¼oz) package active dry yeast
1 cup of warm milk
4 cups all-purpose flour
3 tablespoon sugar
3 tablespoon butter, softened
2 egg yolks
A pinch of salt
Vegetable oil for frying
Confectioner's sugar, to sprinkle
Ground cinnamon, to sprinkle

Cream
2 cups milk
3 tablespoon corn starch
4 egg yolks
½ cup sugar
1 teaspoon vanilla extract
Lime zest, to taste

Preparation
Mix the yeast with the sugar and the milk in a bowl and leave for 5 minutes. Add this mixture and the rest of the prepared dough

ingredients to a stand mixer bowl and mix until they make a smooth dough. Cover and leave this dough for 20 minutes. Knead this dough on a floured surface spread into ½ inch thick sheet. Cut 3 inch rounds from this dough using a cookie cutter. Place these rounds in a greased baking sheet, cover with a kitchen towel, and leave for 30 minutes. Deep fry these dough rounds in hot oil until golden brown. Then remove from the oil and transfer to a plate lined with paper towel. Cut the prepared dough in half. Mix all the cream ingredients in a pan, cook for 10 minutes until it thickens while stirring, and allow the cream to cool. Stuff the cream in between each donut half and dust them with cinnamon and sugar. Serve.

Passion Fruit Mousse

Preparation time: 10 minutes
Nutrition facts (per serving): 141 Cal (10g fat, 2g protein, 1.1g fiber)

Here comes a dessert that's truly loved by all. The passion fruit mousse is a refreshing dessert to serve in summers.

Ingredients (2 servings)
2 teaspoon unflavored gelatin
3 tablespoon water
1 ⅓ cups heavy cream, cold
1 can (14 oz.) sweetened condensed milk
1 cup passion fruit pulp

Topping
Pulp of 2 fresh passion fruits, with seeds
¼ cup sugar

Preparation
Mix the gelatin with water in a bowl and heat for 30 seconds in the microwave. Mix well and blend it with the remaining mousse ingredients in a blender until smooth. Mix the passion fruit with the sugar in a suitable saucepan and cook until soft. Mash and mix well. Garnish the mousse with the passion fruit topping. Serve.

Caipirinha Cocktail

Preparation time: 10 minutes
Nutrition facts (per serving): 218 Cal (8g fat, 4g protein, 1g fiber)

This Brazilian cocktail famous for its blend of lime slices, sugar, cachaça, and lime juice. Enjoy it to beat the heat.

Ingredients (1 serving)
2 limes sliced
2 tablespoon of sugar
2 oz. of cachaca
1 tablespoon of fresh lime juice
Crushed ice

Garnish
Lime slices

Preparation
Mix all the caipirinha cocktail ingredients in a jug. Serve.

Strawberry Caipirinha

Preparation time: 5 minutes
Nutrition facts (per serving): 203 Cal (11g fat, 1g protein, 0g fiber)

The Brazilian strawberry caipirinha drink is all that you need to celebrate the holidays. Keep the ready in your refrigerator for quick serving.

Ingredients (1 serving)
5 quartered medium strawberries, mashed
3 tablespoon granulated sugar
4 tablespoon sparkling water
Crushed ice

Preparation
Mix all the strawberry caipirinha cocktail ingredients in a jug. Serve.

Brazilian Lemonade

Preparation time: 5 minutes
Nutrition facts (per serving): 286 Cal (7g fat, 4g protein, 1g fiber)

Here's a special Brazilian lemonade drink from water, sugar, lime, and condensed milk. Serve fresh for the best taste.

Ingredients (6 servings)
4 juicy limes, washed and scrubbed
6 cups water
1 cup sugar
6 tablespoon sweetened condensed milk

Preparation
Mix all the lemonade ingredients in a jug. Serve.

Brazilian Strawberry Drink

Preparation time: 5 minutes
Nutrition facts (per serving): 207 Cal (1g fat, 1g protein, 1.3g fiber)

Made with strawberry, milk and vodka, this beverage is a refreshing addition to the Brazilian cocktail menu.

Ingredients (2 servings)
½ cup vodka
¼ cup condensed milk
1 teaspoon sugar
2 cups milk
½ box milk cream
¼ cup yogurt
5 strawberries

Preparation
Blend all the Brazilian strawberry drink ingredients in a blender. Serve.

Brazilian Sunrise Cocktail

Preparation time: 10 minutes
Nutrition facts (per serving): 106 Cal (0g fat, 0g protein, 9g fiber)

This refreshing sunrise cocktail is always a delight to serve at parties. Now you can make it easily at home by using the following simple ingredients.

Ingredients (2 servings)
1 oz. cachaca
1 oz. triple sec
1 cup orange juice
2 tablespoons of grenadine
Orange and lime slices for garnish

Preparation
Mix all the sunrise cocktail ingredients in a cocktail shaker. Garnish with orange and lime slices. Serve.

Made in the USA
Middletown, DE
03 December 2024

66014069R00095